PROUDLY WE SPEAK YOUR NAME

FORTY-FOUR YEARS AT LITTLE ROCK CATHOLIC HIGH SCHOOL

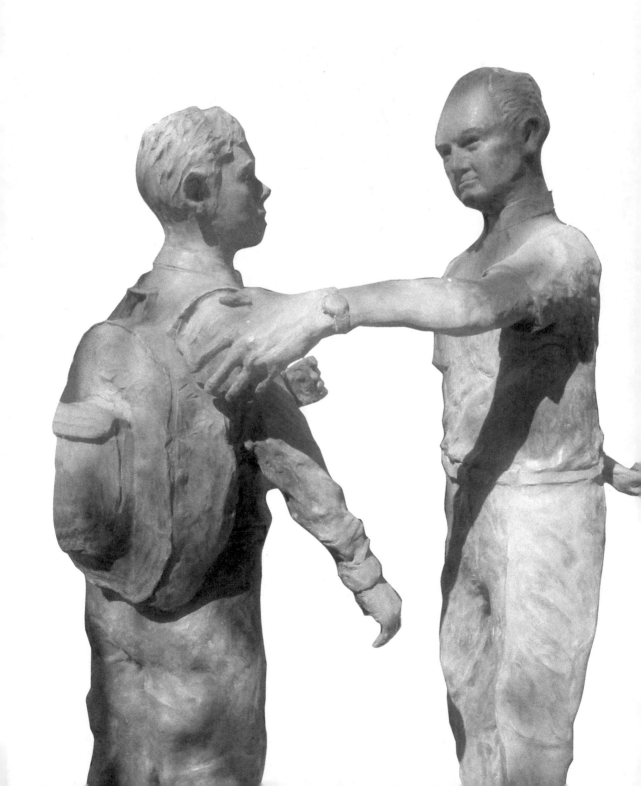

PROUDLY WE SPEAK YOUR NAME

FORTY-FOUR YEARS AT LITTLE ROCK CATHOLIC HIGH SCHOOL

MICHAEL J. MORAN

Butler Center Books

Little Rock, Arkansas

www.butlercenter.org

Printed in the United States of America

First paperback edition, 2016

Library of Congress LCCN: 2008942761

This book is printed on archival-quality paper that meets requirements of the American National Standard for Information Sciences, Permanence of Paper, Printed Library Materials, ANSI Z39.48-1984.

ISBN: 978-1-945624-04-9

Photographs used in this book are the property of the author or were secured for use in this book by the author. Used by permission of Little Rock Catholic High School, Little Rock, Arkansas.

Book design and cover design:	Wendell E. Hall
Page composition:	Shelly Culbertson
Acquired for Butler Center Books by:	David Stricklin and Ted Parkhurst
Project manager and editor:	Ted Parkhurst

DEDICATION:

To Mom and Dad,

Sue and Luci,

John and Cathy

ACKNOWLEDGMENTS:

My sincere thanks to the following: to Roger Armbrust, my friend of fifty-seven years, for his belief that I could and should write this recollection and for facilitating it; to Ted Parkhurst, manager of Butler Center Books, for his expert guidance and judgment; to CHS colleagues and friends Don Lawson and Steve Wells for their assistance in remembering the stories and the facts as best we could recall them; to Charlie Schlumberger, former student and present friend, for legal advice nonpareil; to John Moran, as fine a son as a man could hope to have, for his advice and corrections; and to Cathy Moran, my wife and dearest friend, for her encouragement and love.

CATHOLIC HIGH SCHOOL FOR BOYS ALMA MATER:

Proudly we speak your name,

Proudly wear your colors.

Friendships made within your walls

Will mellow through the years.

We, in some distant day,

May brush away a tear,

Born of memories as these,

We hold so very dear.

—BY MR. THOMAS MORRISSEY, SR.

Bryce Alexander
Aaron Ault
Todd Baker
Hardin Bale
Justin Bank
Christopher Barron

Scott Beard
Matthew Beck
Douglas Becker
Paul Bennett
Daniel Beranek
Joseph Bibb

Thomas Blackmon
Nathan Bramlett
Johnny Branch
Aaron Bromberg
Christopher Brown
Verdell Bunting

Thomas Burnett
Blake Byrd
Andrew Caldwell
Chad Carlson
Mark Carter
Christopher Cascio

Michael Cherry
Thane Chisholm
Richard Cochran
Christopher Colclasure
Matthew Conrad
Christopher Cozart

Just thirty of the 7,000 students the author taught during his forty years on the CHS faculty—from the 1988 yearbook.

First, Some Background:

Catholic High School for Boys was established in Little Rock, Arkansas, in 1930 by Bishop John Morris at 25th and State Streets, where Little Rock College and then St. John's Seminary had formerly been located. In January 0f 1961, CHS moved to 6300 Lee Avenue (now Father Tribou Street). The first graduating class of 1931 numbered five. Since then, more than 7000 students have become alumni.

Father George Tribou is the towering figure in Catholic High history. Coming to Little Rock from Jenkintown, Pennsylvania, George Tribou was ordained a priest for the diocese of Little Rock and in the second year of his priesthood was assigned to CHS, where he served as teacher and principal for more than fifty years, until his death in 2001. Any recollection of Catholic High School would be incomplete without recognition of the centrality of Father Tribou's role in defining its character. Even when elevated to the position of Monsignor in his later years, he preferred to be called "Father," a role he played in the lives of untold numbers of Catholic High boys.

In many places in this account he will be referred to as "Father T," a name with which I was accustomed to address him.

I, Michael Moran, of the class of 1961, began to teach at my alma mater in 1968. During my career I taught English, Religion, Latin, World History, National Problems, Introductory Mathematics, and Driver Education. I ended my teaching career at the school in May of 2008.

By Way of Introduction:

To those who have not known Catholic High School boys first-hand, the image of us over the last forty or more years has been most easily characterized by our externals: We have short hair, wear khaki pants, dress shirts, and ties from the September celebration of the Senior Ring Mass until the heat of springtime (though old boys are agitated to hear that shorts can be worn when the temperature is above 90 degrees), and, above all, do not have the civilizing influence of female classmates. And as far as any generalization can go to capture the reality of the school, that's as good as any.

But no one, no matter how much time he or she spends in the presence of Catholic High and its boys, can entirely capture our essence. We are too many and too varied. Some of us look back on our Catholic High days with disgruntlement; others recall the experience with great satisfaction. The responses to the place and its culture are disparate; it is a situation that calls for recognition of the subjective nature of the experience. Each of us who attended had his own "Catholic High experience," as Father Tribou so often called it.

So what follows is just one Catholic High boy's recollections of the school, which was my alma mater after four years and my employer for forty years.

I began as a ninety-eight pounder (according to my freshman-football weigh-in) at age thirteen. Scholastically I was somewhere in the top ten, though not one of the stars, academically speaking. I was fairly good at Algebra but puzzled throughout most of Geometry, Trigonometry, Chemistry and Physics. My best class was English, and I won a small cup at graduation for my ability. I always liked to write what Father Tribou called a "theme," a weekly assignment, though it wasn't until I was finished with it that I could write the outline he wanted us to include. I always felt a bit guilty about that, knowing that his directive was surely the proper way to go about the business of composing. (I have a tinge of that old feeling now as I realize that I have no clear idea here at the outset about how this recollection will take shape.) I loved basketball as a boy and played four years at Catholic High, not getting a starting role until I was a senior. We had a good season and got to the semi-finals of the state tournament played at Barton Coliseum. My classmates and I, the class of 1961, were the first to graduate from the Lee Street address. That made for a never-to-be-forgotten conclusion to our careers. When I returned to teach seven years later, I had never spent a day in a classroom being in charge. Leaving nothing to chance, I wrote out every word of my first day's class in 1968. Now, sparked again by my association with CHS, I write to try to capture what Eudora Welty called "the elusive atmosphere of place."

MY CATHOLIC HIGH—
1957 TO 1961:

My forty-four years at Catholic High School for Boys were a surprise to me. I used to joke, even after fifteen or twenty years on the job, "I still haven't decided what I want to be when I grow up." But now I know that all I really wanted to be was a teacher. I never seriously or for long considered anything else. One could chalk that up to my lack of imagination, or the power that inertia exercised over me, but I believe instead that it's a case of finding what one loves to do and being smart enough to stay with it. I have recommended the profession, to students who have expressed interest in it, for one abiding characteristic: No two days are ever alike. The variety presented by a classroom teeming with teen-aged boys is enough to stimulate anyone's interest. And if one's attention should wane from the task at hand, the penalties extracted by those whom one is supposed to be teaching are swift and unpredictable. The simile I used to describe teaching to myself (and occasionally to another teacher) was that it was like boxing: One needed to come out swinging or else one would get beaten up. That's not to say that I thought of students as opponents. I viewed them as a natural force that could be turned to beneficial use only if properly channeled. I had to learn how to do that—from the start of every period to the end. But before I could take up that career path, there was the matter of growing up that had to be taken care of.

*****

As a first and second grade student at St. Peter's (before the apostrophe and S were expelled from Catholic institutions) in Kirkwood, Missouri, if I ever gave any thought to going to high school, it would have been to Coyle High, a Catholic co-ed school just across the street from St. Peter's and the place where my sisters went.

If you remember Bob Newhart's second TV show in which he played an inn-keeper, you may recall that one character had two brothers named Darryl. Well, I had two sisters named Mary. My devout Catholic parents, Grace and Raymond Moran, named both daughters for the Blessed Virgin— thus, Mary Susan and Mary Lucille, nine and seven years older than I, respectively, and known to me as Sue and Luci. My sisters told me that as a child I wasn't the easiest "little brother" a sister ever had (a term both of them used occasionally to address me into adulthood). Despite my orneriness, I recall both of them patiently trying to teach me how to spell my name, a feat that I doubted I should ever accomplish, but as good teachers they persisted until I finally succeeded.

In 1951 my parents announced to the three of us that we were moving. Southwestern Bell had work for my father to do in Little Rock, Arkansas. Geographically challenged, I had never heard of Arkansas, much less Little Rock. Sue was to be a senior in high school and desperately wanted to stay in Kirkwood to graduate from Coyle. We had a loving aunt, my dad's sister Lucille Steffen, who agreed to let Sue stay with her if she could get my parents to agree. My mother, a very gracious woman in the opinion of many, me included, nevertheless had a way of stopping some arguments before they started. Perhaps it was a look, or a tone of voice, or just her succinctness that let one know that further conversation on the point was useless. That's apparently what Sue heard when Mom said, "The family is moving." And so we did, all of us, in the summer of 1951.

Not having been born in Little Rock, I became aware of Catholic High School for Boys belatedly. My first knowledge of it was that Luci, as a senior at Mt. St. Mary's (old style!) in 1953, had become something called a "cheerleader" for Catholic High. My lack of information about the world extended far beyond geography, and that included what a cheerleader was or did. Whatever a cheerleader was, my sister was one, and so the name of CHS had entered my slowly enlarging vocabulary.

My second clear memory about Catholic High came when I was about in the sixth grade. One of my schoolmates asked, "Do you know what L.S.M.F.T. stands for?" Just about any kid, even one so out-of-touch as I, had that one covered. The American Tobacco Company's advertizing had drummed it into just about everybody's head that the acronym stood for "Lucky Strike means fine tobacco." And so I confidently informed him. "That's not what it means," he gleefully replied. "It means 'Lord, save me from Tribou.'"

I was thus introduced to Tribou, Father Tribou, that is. Clearly his reputation among even grade-schoolers was scary, though it was not exactly clear to me for what he should be feared. It strikes me now as more than bit ironic, five decades after first hearing that forewarning about Father Tribou, that (so I have been told) similar ominous tales had been passed on about me by parochial school boys of a certain age. But back in 1955 I was still a couple of years away from finding out first-hand about Catholic High School for Boys and the fearsome Father Tribou. And speaking of *fearsome*, the mighty "Wabbit" of Our Lady of the Holy Souls School, the mascot of its athletic teams, is what I concentrated on most for the next couple of years, as my life revolved around football (as a sidearm-slinging QB) and basketball (a short, slow guard whose best moments came after I passed to another player). When my days as a Wabbit were over, it was time to go to high school.

*****

When I began the ninth grade at Catholic High, I lived on Longwood, in Cammack Village, a little, independent enclave on the northwest edge of Little Rock. Cammack Village, I've been told, was mostly a post-WW II creation. Ours was a house like most of the others: probably three-bedrooms at most and clapboard of various hues. From Longwood I usually got to CHS's downtown location in the south central part of the city at 2500 State by bus, with the Main Street local being my trip in the morning and the Pulaski Heights line my return. I estimate the trip took about 25 minutes each way, leaving a fair amount of time to do some last-minute studying or chatting with my chums who were also CHS-bound. The public transportation system of Little Rock played a significant part in my first two years of high school, just as it had been the focus of eye-opening experiences when I first moved to Little Rock.

When I migrated to LR at age eight, I was shocked by the southern determination to keep white and black citizens apart. It was mostly from my mother that the customs of this place called Arkansas were explained, and thus, little by little, I derived an understanding of the various taboos and traditions that held the system together. The sign of enforced segregation that I saw each day going by bus to Catholic High was the written rule posted on every bus that the back of the vehicle was the only place for the "colored" to sit or stand. To add to the written rule, a line on the floor about two-thirds of the way to the back was the demarcation point that all riders had to observe. Everybody knew his or her place. For a child reared in the St. Louis area, about 350 miles north, the system was puzzling and, even to one so imperceptive about other worldly matters, wrong.

I saw that there were no Negro students in my grade school at Holy Souls or any at Catholic High. I had memories of an integrated classroom at St. Peter's in Kirkwood, but the segregation in the Catholic Schools I attended in Little Rock didn't strike me as being offensive the way the line on the bus floor did. I remember thinking that the segregated Catholic school system in Little Rock, with St. Augustine's and St. Bartholomew's being the grade school and high school for Negroes, was probably the best that the Catholic diocese could manage; that judgment was based more on wishful thinking than on any facts in my possession. My parents were early members of the Catholic Interracial Council in Little Rock, a group formed to begin making connections between divided communities. I remember that when a picture of the group was going to be taken for publication in *The Guardian*, the local Catholic newspaper, someone warned my father that such a photo could be harmful to his career. Dad's reply, "I don't give a damn," was something of which I have always been proud. Integration in Catholic schools in Little Rock and North Little Rock finally began in the mid-1960s. Having graduated by then, I don't know details of the process, but if no news is, indeed, good news, then it was presumably a smooth transition, given that I've never heard a word about any opposition or trouble when it took place.

*****

I started at Catholic High the day after Labor Day in 1957, and I was one of perhaps 250 students in the school. Our ninth grade class had about eighty students, making us the biggest class there to date. The physical appearance of Catholic High then, both in the location and in the students themselves, was strikingly different from that of the first decade of the twenty-first century. The buildings at 25th and State were three: classrooms (and quarters for two priests, the principal and the assistant) in one, the gym in another, and the third was the library. The buildings exhibited a tired-looking, red brick exterior, and the marble stairs in the classroom building had little puddles of wear in them from countless feet of Little Rock College and St. John's Seminary students who had preceded us in the edifice. Out front, on a pedestal, stood a statue of an American Doughboy, a World War I soldier. The statue was dedicated to the students of Little Rock College who had served and died in the war. The statue's vintage only added to the antiquity that we perceived about our premises.

The halls in the classroom building were extremely narrow, even for the passage of fewer than three hundred students. The six-foot tall lockers were halved, with freshmen assigned to the lower section. We newcomers squatted to retrieve our books at our own jeopardy, as knocking us over with well placed knees seemed an organized sport among seniors. Oh, to be a sophomore and elevated to an upper locker!

Speaking of seniors, they ruled this small roost and emphasized their status by invoking the ancient rite of Initiation, which was a week-long test. Depending on the senior to whom the newcomer was assigned, Initiation was either a rigorous test or an almost unnoticed phenomenon. The seniors approached it with varying degrees of enthusiasm, innovation, and aspiring cruelty. I was one of the lucky ones—my "big brother," a glasses-wearing, slight, scholarly looking, serene fellow named John Robinson, had little or nothing for me to do to prove my worth as a new CHS student. Other frosh were not so fortunate. I recall seeing a few down on all-fours, using their noses to push the proverbial peanut across the CHS playground, a clay-colored, dust-ridden hardpan. The seniors who relished their roles as tormentors marched their blindfolded charges into the gym building, whose bottom floor was bathrooms, dressing rooms, and an alleged swimming pool. Once into the bathroom area, the unhappy few whom fate had caused to fall into the hands of the Twelfth-Graders from Hades had to kneel and embrace at close range toilet bowls brimming with Limburger cheese. I was told the cheese smelled very little like cheese. The whole Initiation ritual, which had begun Monday morning, ended at noon Friday, with some brief ceremony on the playing field welcoming us into the brotherhood. It's fair to say that some of us freshmen felt more brotherly to the seniors than did others.

*****

One class that I remember vividly my freshman year was Coach Mike Malham's Civics class. Coach Malham was a force not to be ignored. He was, to the best of my figuring, about thirty-three at that time, full of vigor, in the full strength of all his powers, and renowned as a dynamic and demanding figure both in athletics and in the classroom. Apparently two of my fellow freshmen had not gotten the word on Coach Malham's status: he who is to be obeyed.

One of these lads sat right in front of me, the other just to his left. They were chatting whilst the coach was teaching. Just as I was thinking that they were not showing very good judgment, Coach Malham bounded down from the slightly raised platform on which his desk was placed and all but ran down the isle to the two miscreants. Let it be said that in the late fifties, corporal punishment at Catholic High was an everyday event. On this day it involved two handfuls of hair being grabbed, and the heads to which that hair was attached being brought together swiftly. Sitting as close as I was, I thought then and have long remembered that the sound made me think of coconuts being banged together (though I'd never actually heard such a thing). To say that good order in Coach Malham's class was a constant for the rest of the year is to state the obvious. We all had a memorable learning experience that day.

Fridays were "Current Events" days in Coach Malham's Civics class. It was the job of each of us to cut out from that morning's *Arkansas Gazette* or the previous night's *Arkansas Democrat* an article that one could describe to the class. The article was to be glued or taped to a piece of notebook paper and a summary of it was to be included, a summary that one might be chosen to present orally to the class—from memory. As I mentioned earlier, I did some homework on the bus on my way to school many times—but always on Friday. Those of us who lived in my area and rode the bus would share a morning or evening paper, scissors, and tape, as we hurried to get our current event ready for Coach Malham.

Coach Malham would take up all the papers with current events on them, choose papers seemingly at random, and began to call on us to deliver our reports. He was usually helpful if one were to forget some details, so the pressure wasn't great to perform. One day, however, he heard something he didn't like.

My incongruously named classmate Dutch O'Neal was picked to speak about his current event. He stood before us, hands behind his back, seeming pleased to get a chance to bring us up-to-date. He began: "Yesterday blonde bombshell movie star Jayne Mansfield married Hungarian weightlifter Mickey Hargitay in a ceremony..."

"Son! We don't need to hear about that sort of thing," boomed an obviously angry Mike Malham. Dutch was surprised at the interruption and

For a freshman, surviving the onslaughts in the cramped hallway at 25th and State made Initiation Week seem like it lasted a year.

stood quietly and looked wonderingly at Coach Malham. "Sit down, son!" he was ordered. As Dutch sadly went to his place, it's likely we all made mental note to consider more carefully the content of future "Current Events."

*****

The appearance of Catholic High boys has for several decades been uniform: short hair, khaki pants, a dress shirt, and a tie. While there are variations on this because of season of the year (shorts and polo shirts in the heat of August, September, and May) and class level (for several years seniors have had a distinctive sports coat or sweater to wear), the CHS student is generally recognizable by his neat appearance. But it has not always been so.

When I began at Catholic High, there was a significant contingent with a look that might surprise today's students. The duck-tail hairdo was popular in the middle and late fifties. This coiffure was created with the help of a slippery substance like Wildroot Cream Oil, or a pomade like Vaseline that kept the "wings" of the duck in place on the back of the head and also aided in the formation and retention of a curl that dangled in mid-forehead. Henry Winkler's version of this look as Fonzie in the TV series *Happy Days* was a replica of the real thing at CHS. The duck-tail virtually demanded an accompanying wardrobe accessory: a black, leather jacket. And CHS lads had them—not that they were the dominant expression of the student body fashion sense, but enough in evidence to indicate the ongoing influence of actor Marlon Brando in his anti-establishment role in *The Wild One*, a 1953 motorcycle-gang movie that set the style for multitudes of American boys. We had some rebellious-looking characters in our midst, though probably not more than one in ten. They were perceived as "hoods," to use the term popular at the time. In truth, I never knew one to be a bully or to cause trouble, but their look had a powerful effect on one's judgment.

Not all of us were emulating Brando, and for us the usual outfit tended more to what had been our usual grade-school choices: plaid flannel shirts and blue jeans. While these two selections would have prompted little in the way of critical comment from adults (who weren't generally enthusiastic about the counter-culture motorcycle-gang look), the outfit was, nevertheless, anything but the stylish garb that came to characterize succeeding generations of Catholic High students. It's my recollection that the change in the appearance of the typical CHS student began after the move to the new school at 6300 Lee. I don't know if the new look was the result of an administrative decision reached by then-principal Father William Galvin to require a standard outfit that would be in keeping with the splendid new school, or might have been occasioned by Father Tribou's becoming principal in the mid-sixties. However it began, all who attended CHS then or thereafter would agree that Father Tribou had an image of Catholic High that he imposed upon the school and its students as the years progressed. The sweater that seniors now wear was a direct result of Father Tribou's seeing a photo in the *New York Times* of some Catholic high school students from that area who were so dressed. He told me, "I want our boys to look like that." What I am certain of is that by the time I returned to teach in 1968, having graduated seven years before, the new "look" was firmly established. When Father Tribou spoke of the CHS dress code, he always said essentially the same thing: "The way you dress says something about the seriousness of the activity in which you are engaged. We think school is serious business, so you should dress accordingly." And so Catholic High boys have worn their distinctive threads for more than forty years.

*****

One highlight of my freshman year was the outstanding Rocket football team. The Rockets won ten games and lost one, and like a many a freshman before and since, I marveled at the Rockets' home field, which was War Memorial Stadium. Besides the Rockets, the only other regular user of War Memorial was the Razorback team of the University of Arkansas. I don't know if I thought the Rockets' ten wins were so terrific at the time; I may have thought that such was the usual at CHS, but having the vantage point of fifty years, now I can see how extraordinary that team was. The players I was most aware of at the time had the glamour positions: Ronnie Pyle was the scatback touchdown-maker; Buddy Cagle was a rangy end who caught most of the passes thrown by Tom Barre, the quarterback who led the team.

Ronnie Pyle once had the distinction of needing twelve guys to tackle him. In one game where he had already run one punt return back for a touchdown, he got loose on another and was streaking down the sidelines with Cagle to block for him and nobody in sight to make the tackle. That's when the opponent's twelfth man took over. A frustrated substitute who apparently couldn't bear the sight of Ronnie being goalward-bound again jumped off the bench and on to the field, knocking Pyle off his feet, a bizarre sight, but one seen just three years before during the Cotton Bowl game when Dickey Maegle from Rice was similarly taken down.

Both Pyle and Cagle knew at once what violation of the rules had occurred, and they pointed at the illegal tackler. The referee sized up the situation quickly, and standing there on the thirty-five yard line, he threw both hands over his head signaling yet another Rocket six points. It was an unforgettable moment in an unforgettable season.

*****

The sophomore year is always a relief. Now some other tyros have to bear the burden of being the new kids who have so much to learn about the place and their place in it. (And sophomores didn't have to have bottom lockers!) One especially delightful person who first came to my attention in that year was Father John Doyle. Like Father Tribou and several other priests in the Little Rock diocese, Father Doyle hailed from the general area of Philadelphia, a diocese so rich in vocations that it could afford to suggest to some of its young would-be priests that they might like the challenge of a far-away place called Little Rock. So Father Doyle was a dang Yankee, but his effervescent personality was hard to resist. He was jolly, smart, athletic, and had a million jokes—not only to tell, but to play.

My basketball brother was Roger Armbrust. Friends since I moved to LR in '51, we spent huge chunks of time playing ball; if we had given half that time to practicing the piano or cello, we'd have made it to Carnegie Hall. We went to CHS one winter Saturday to play in the gym, inhospitably small and cold though it might have been. And who should show up to play? Father Doyle! We hadn't tested his mettle on the court prior to that morning, and we and some others were engaged in a game of three-on-three as we began to see him reveal his repertoire of Philly-style roundball. I'm guessing that at the time that he was taking on us fifteen-year-olds he must have been in his mid-thirties. He showed us quickly that he knew his way around the hardwood, especially when it came to making adroit passes to his teammates for easy score. Roger was on his side, and as he was the recipient of one of Fr. Doyle's fancy assists, he couldn't contain his enthusiasm for the excellent pass: "Atta boy...uh, Father!" A man who could play like that and be a priest too was a potent combination.

Father Doyle taught biology. He was the kind of teacher who would cackle after he asked, "Moran, what is the anther?" and I pretended to lisp, "Father, what wath the quethtion?" It was in biology, of course, that the specimen jar

The sartorial styles of the late 1950s clash with the modern look.

of formaldehyde-soaked creatures would be examined through dissection. On the day when we were dissecting a mussel, one of the budding scientists called out loudly, "Father Doyle, I found a pearl!"

Father Doyle went rushing back to the lad's desk and soon was exulting for all to hear about the discovery. One or two skeptical student comments were heard, something about mussels not producing pearls. Then the ecstatic discoverer noticed that his "pearl" had tiny holes in each end, as if it had been recently liberated from a dime- store necklace. Father Doyle had worked his sleight-of-hand, (though he never openly took "credit" for depositing the gem). The Joker had struck; we later were told that ours wasn't the first class to have a mussel surrender a pearl.

*****

One event of the second year that sticks with me, mentally not physically, was the day of the paddling. A certain priest, unhappy with our classroom decorum, invited his second-period class to stay after school for an indeterminate period of time, something no teacher would dream of doing today. What is also not dreamed of in this era is the widespread use of the "board of education" to teach lessons in deportment.

But this was 1958, and spared rods were few and far between. As we sat in confused anticipation of what Father So-and-so was going to do, he ended the speculation by walking briskly into the room with paddle in hand. He said nothing at first, just looked us over. Then he pointed at one of the thirty of us and said, "You, come with me."

As they disappeared into the hall, the thought crossed my mind that it all might be a charade. Perhaps they would both return quickly, and Father would ask if we had learned a lesson. Instead, we all heard the sizzling crack of the paddle against something. (Surely that wasn't the derriere of our classmate!) Two more blows followed, and in a moment our initiate came back to the room unsteadily, with tears in his eyes. Scratch the charade theory.

Then another boy was called out—and another three whacks rang out. Jim Lipsmeyer, a short, slender fellow but with an extremely high pain threshold, was sitting right in front of me when he was called. When he came back and another victim was marched out, I leaned forward and whispered, "Was it bad?" His gasped words, "Oh, God!" were enough for me. Prayers to whatever god saves one from a beating were immediately formed in my heart—but to no avail. I was next.

As I followed Father Paddler into the hall, I thought he looked a little fatigued. Perhaps the licks would be less stinging than the ones so far delivered. "Bend over and grab your ankles, Mo. But before you do, take out your wallet—I want you to get the full effect," he said in an oddly emotionless voice. My hope that he was tiring was dashed by the first smack. Wow! It stung like a thousand needles. It did, though, have the anesthetic effect of making the next two less painful, and I managed to wobble back to my place.

One unifying thing about the paddling was that none of us had given the priest any satisfaction (if he was looking for it) by crying out in pain. He could beat us, but he couldn't make us yelp! That is, until a lad was called out who had transferred to CHS that year and apparently didn't get the macho memo about showing no pain. When he took his first lick, he bleated like one of Mary's lambs. We who had been popped, and even those who hadn't and still were in torment as to whether they would be next, had a hard time not laughing out loud.

After ten or so fellows had taken their licks, the priest came in and asked if lessons had been learned, blah, blah, blah. We all averred that they had, and we probably didn't misbehave much, if at all, in his class from then on. But I have no fond recollection of the day, no yearning for the "good old days" when boys could be walloped and when very few people, including parents, ever dared to ask if such was a good way to discipline children. In my view, one may, if he chooses, contemplate some mild corporal punishment for his own children of a certain age who lack understanding or appreciation of verbal corrections, but hitting other people's children doesn't seem to me to be instructive—or necessary.

*****

My junior year memories of things scholastic have to do with a first-year teacher by the name of Mr. Marion Mortensen. He was, I found out years later, sixty years old when he taught us Algebra II. Had you asked us his age, we'd have probably guessed eighty. Soft-spoken, somewhat slow moving, Mr. Mortensen was not exactly what you'd choose as your model for a new teacher to tackle some very experienced juniors. His ability to discipline us depended more on our mood than his methods. Our bad behavior wasn't outrageous, but it must have been distracting to him to hear the hum of muffled conversation as he tried to get on with his lesson.

Mr. Mortensen wasn't a Catholic, so he deferred to various students to begin the class with the traditional prayer. The leader of the prayer would commonly follow it with a brief invocation such as "Mary, Queen of Peace," to which the rest of us responded, "Pray for us." Well, we took advantage of Mr. Mortensen even when we were praying, as we heard an imaginative fellow cite a popular song of the day in his invocation: "Queen of the Hop," to which we loudly and delightedly replied, "Pray for us!" "Hula Hoop Mistress" on another day got the same hearty response. We were having a bit of fun at old Mr. Mortensen's expense.

But then something happened as the year went by. The man's basic goodness somehow started to wear away at our crassness and disrespect. When he corrected us for misbehavior, it was always gently done. His kindness and his earnest desire to do his job managed to overcome our youthful insensitivity and lack of self-restraint. Mr. Mortensen had a saying that he used time and again when we got a problem right. He would proclaim, "I'll buy that!" As the year progressed we sought to evoke that response. We wanted to succeed and get his approval. I fondly recall him now, fifty years later, for what we learned from him about the power of goodness and gentleness and devotion to duty. Thank you, Mr. Mortensen, for those important lessons.

*****

A junior, though considered an upperclassman, still may be in awe of his older brothers, the seniors. The class of 1960 was well endowed with admirable types of fellows: scholars, athletes, and personality-plus types. These boys populated the last class that would spend all four years at the downtown CHS, and they left a mighty mark on the school. Our class didn't likely eclipse the boys of '60 except in one respect: dancing.

This is not to defame all of the '60 fellows, but it was odd for a class with so many gifted athletes and social butterflies that the same bunch had so many left feet. It isn't much of a claim to fame for those of us of the class of 1961, but I would still affirm that objective watchers of the Terpsichorean talents of the two classes would give the nod to us. I know we had more guys appear on *Steve's Show*, the popular after-school dance party that ruled the airwaves for several years in Little Rock. So, take that, '60!

*****

It was in my junior year that I came much more deeply to know the person of Catholic High's coach of both football and basketball, Mr. Mike

Malham. I had already learned, from my time spent with him, first as a freshman in his Civics class and then as a sophomore football player (a career cut short, mercifully, by a broken arm), that he was a taskmaster nonpareil. Perhaps if Coach Malham had just explained to us what he probably thought we already understood, namely, that his rigorous conditioning was going to put us in better physical shape than any opponent we faced, it might have been easier to bear his demanding ways. He probably thought we were smart enough to figure out for ourselves that no other team spent as much time as the Rockets did, either in the round- or pointed-ball sport, doing all the draining work that it took to get into peak physical condition.

And if he had told us that his interminable running of plays in practice, both in football and basketball—the same plays over and over—would give us the edge when crucial situations arose, it might have made the mind-numbing repetition less onerous. But again, he likely assumed we were clever enough to realize that. Is there any player who ever was tutored in either sport by Coach Malham who can't recall vividly these words: "Run it again!"?

Though Mike Malham had some extraordinary teams, such as the 10-1 football squad in 1957, and state basketball tournament semi-finalists in 1960, what I remember most about him now is what he taught us about sportsmanship. One incident I experienced as a basketball player when I was a junior stands out in my mind. One team we were playing was badly outclassed by our starters. We had some terrific senior players that year, Larry Hoyt and Joe Breyel chief among them. For those of us who were secondteamers, we were licking our chops by halftime at the prospect of spelling the first-stringers and getting some significant playing time ourselves.

Sure enough, about halfway through the third quarter Coach Malham called out the names of us subs and told us we were going in. The rout was on by that time; we were winning by more than twenty points. Just before the five fresh subs were about to go into the game, he called us to him.

"Boys, we have these fellows beaten. So we're not going to rub it in. Before you shoot the ball, be sure that we have passed the ball at least ten times. If you've got a layup, and we haven't passed that many times, you'd better not take it, because if you do, I'm going to take you out and you won't get back in the game."

As highly disappointed as those instructions made me at the time, to the same degree they now sing the praises of Mike Malham, who had compassion for another team and its coach and taught me and everyone else a valuable lesson, though I was certainly slow to understand it. Mike Malham was a great coach in many ways.

*****

My senior year has so many vivid memories that it's hard to control my tendency to prolixity in discussing them—but I'll try. Our move to Lee Street into our extraordinary new school is certainly at the top of the list. Bishop Albert Fletcher had approved the construction of the place, and he presided over the formal dedication on Sunday, February 26, 1961.

We seniors were given the task at that auspicious occasion of enlightening those who were touring the school about its wonders. Each of us had a

My friends since 1951, Steve Schubert (left) and Jerry Joe Harrison, escort the 1960 Homecoming Queen Cathy Wortsmith (more about her in the "Graduation 2008" section). At the Homecoming Dance, the class of '61 skillfully danced the night away!

particular part of the building to describe to the visitors who passed by our designated areas. My job was to praise the "terrazzo" floors of the lobby and first floor—though I had no idea what the term meant. The floors *were* nice and shiny!

After Bishop Fletcher blessed the building, Father Galvin had appointed me to make a special request, odd though it may seem: Would the bishop declare the following day as a day off from school? Father Galvin hadn't told me of the role I was to play until shortly before I was to speak. This was a request that was to be part of the program—lots of folks would presumably be listening to my words. I did a bit of cogitation, and when the time came to speak, I made the request for the day off, somehow shoehorning the word *magnanimous* into my description of Bishop Fletcher. I thought it was a complimentary term, but why I chose to try it out on that occasion I don't know. He laughed when he heard me say it, and I was sure I had made a big mistake. Then he thanked me for my generous depiction and said it had been a long time since anybody called him "magnanimous." I really needn't tell you that Bishop Fletcher was a very kind man! And, yes, he did grant the free day.

*****

There's a plaque on the wall opposite the cafeteria that commemorates the Rockets' first game in the new gymnasium on the 4th of February, and it reflects the fact that we won by a score of 34-33 over North Little Rock. The capacity crowd of eight hundred took my breath away when I walked out with my teammates to warm up for the game. No Rocket team in history had ever played a home game to so many people. It was a thrilling night.

Our coach was Happy Mahfouz, himself an excellent college player, and yet one who had reasonable expectations for his high school players. Coach Mahfouz presided over what were my worst and best moments on the court as a Rocket. Once when a junior B teamer, I was dribbling the ball up court, uncontested after the other team had scored. All nine players had crossed the half court line as I leisurely approached it. That was when I bounced the ball off my foot. As it began to roll to the sideline, I scrambled after it, too frantically I suppose, because just as I was about to catch up to it, I stumbled and fell, reaching in vain for the ball as it rolled out of bounds—and between Coach Mahfouz's feet as he sat on the sidelines. From my vantage point, that of one whose belly is on the floor, I looked up into his eyes, expecting the worst, and he just shook his head, as if to say, "I've seen everything now!" And he never mentioned it to me afterwards. He was an excellent coach (leading us to 22 victories and the semi-finals of the state tournament)—and a forgiving man!

*****

The cloud that hangs over those wonderful first few months at the new Catholic High is the drowning death of our classmate Burch Raley at the annual senior picnic in Hot Springs. Gil Gerard, our classmate and future actor, tried to the point of exhaustion to revive Burch, but it was to no avail. Burch was the strongest boy in our class, and that strength was matched by his gentleness. When our class meets for reunions, and we mention the loss of our friends, his is the name with which we always start. May he and they continue their peaceful rest.

*****

The class of '61 had its graduation on the last day of May, and the seventy of us represented the largest class in CHS history, a claim to fame that lasted one year. In the succeeding years, the fortunes of Catholic High School for Boys began to develop to the point that some graduating classes had a hundred more members than did ours. On May 31 of 1961, we, the newest members of the alumni of Catholic High School, could hardly have imagined what was to come for our Alma Mater.

FACULTY AND STAFF—
THEN AND NOW:

Father Tribou had a theory about teaching. He said it was often like a delayed explosive that would go off long after the fuse had been ignited. When students are in school, they can't know what teachers will have the most profound effect on their lives—or even the ones they will remember clearly years down the road. These things are not predictable at the time they are being experienced. What follows are some of my memories of some teachers with whom I've worked and of those who taught me. I have no clear idea of why certain things stuck with me and others didn't. It's all very idiosyncratic, I know, and I apologize in advance for my failures of memory, inaccuracies, and omissions.

*****

Who ends up in a classroom at Catholic High School for Boys? The array is vast: from many priests, one nun (Sister Scholastica Vogelpohl, who was a stellar English teacher who gave me tons of good advice—and only when solicited), and one brother (teacher of Religion and Romantic languages, counselor, and irrepressible punster, Brother Richard Sanker) to the parade of non-clerical men and women of multiple types. The prologue to *The*

Canterbury Tales by Geoffrey Chaucer comes to my mind as I consider this cavalcade of teachers. Chaucer picked a group with one obvious thing in common: All were making a pilgrimage to the place of Thomas Becket's martyrdom. Chaucer's genius was his ability to show their individuality. This talent no one should hope to reproduce. Instead I would venture, based on forty-four years of experience, to generalize rather than specify. Above all, my sister and brother teachers have been diligent. I have seen them devote extraordinary efforts to their jobs, which means to their students. I know teachers who show up early for school each day to offer extra help to students; teachers who grade papers as soon as they can, thinking that immediate feedback is helpful; teachers who spend countless hours coaching athletics, putting together yearbooks and newspapers, mentoring would-be thespians, leading the ROTC, heading up clubs like Philosophy, Theology, Beta, R.E.A.C.H., Mu Alpha Theta, and Radio, sponsoring the skit cheerleaders, organizing the TV crew, preparing students for competitions like Quiz Bowl, Model U.N., and the Fed Challenge; teachers who teach each period from start to finish, not cheating their students out of time they could be learning; teachers who lead students to Europe; teachers who aggressively monitor study halls so that the most learning can take place; teachers who take seriously their duty to supervise students at lunch and assemblies; and teachers who take their charges, such as band members, on extracurricular trips. So much of this work is voluntary! So much is done with only one thing in mind: The students will benefit. Their devotion has never failed to impress and encourage me. Having had employment in various sectors myself, I classify my CHS colleagues as easily the hardest working in my experience. I salute the women and men who have tackled this job. It can be very challenging. They have worked diligently at it and have done their work well.

*****

Father Reuben Groff, who taught me U.S. History, was a kind soul whose first choice of priestly ministry, I would have guessed, was probably not teaching. Nonetheless, like other priests of that era, he was assigned (sentenced?) to Catholic High as a teacher. Even Father Groff's dearest relatives, having spent an hour or two in class with him as teacher, would surely admit that he wasn't the most exciting of instructors. Almost all of what went on in our American history class was students reading from the text. He occasionally punctuated the mention of a name by affixing "Old" to it. So I can recall him saying, "Old Sam Adams…" as if they had been pals. The fact that Father Groff was on such good terms with them seemed to me to humanize the famous figures that marched through the pages of our text.

His only other departure from the classroom reading was that sometimes, and for no apparent reason (though perhaps it was to keep himself awake as one of us droned on from the book), he would get up out of his desk, go to the board, and write an important figure's name or that of a historical event, someone or something that had just been mentioned in the reading. When we were in the first few weeks of our class with Father Groff, this dramatic departure from the ordinary course of things—scooting back his chair, rising from it as he grasped a piece of chalk—was initially viewed as having great significance. We would rise from our torpor long enough to write the personage's name or the occasion in our notebooks, thinking it would possibly be a point of importance on examinations. Since we were essentially just reading from the text, our notebooks had little in them save for this occasional highlighting by Father Groff.

We eventually learned from studying this list of unrelated names and events, despite not seeing any significance in or connection between its various elements, that it held no special educational significance. Those facts were not emphasized on tests or in any way made to stand out from the welter of information that survey courses contain. So what few notes we took, triggered by Father Groff's extraordinary excursions to the board, were essentially a waste of lead, paper, and time.

Note-taking became virtually extinct in Father Groff's class. This would have been universally true but for one student: Ferdinand ("Ferdie" to us) Kaczka. Ferdie took notes in a stenographer's notebook, a slender volume, perhaps five by nine inches, presumably shaped to assist in the speed of note-taking. I said that Ferdie took his notes in "a" notebook—make that *many* notebooks. He took notes like mad, as if a loved one's life depended on it. He was a dervish, day in and day out. There was no stopping Ferdie. We insisted that he explain. "Why do you take so many notes?" Ferdie was as succinct as he was diligent: "To stay awake."

For the rest of us, staying awake in Father Groff's history class became either an ongoing, usually fruitless, and always Titanic battle with Morpheus, or a gentle surrender, characterized not by the raising of one's hands, but by the lowering the head to the desk. Ferdie's desire not only to fight the battle, but to win it, seemed quixotic (before we knew the meaning of *quixotic*) to the rest of us.

But Ferdie had his day, and we, his less diligent classmates, finally understood the purpose of his labors. Apparently Ferdie studied his multitude of steno notes, written in his florid but difficult-to-read Palmer cursive, or else the notes made his studying the text all the easier. Ferdie had the highest grade in Father Groff's history class—both semesters.

*****

I'm told that Father Groff was victimized in his first year as a teacher, indeed in his first days on the job. This occurred at the old school on State Street. Father Groff was in charge of a study hall. It held perhaps seventy-five students at a time. Unbeknownst to him the study hall had a door at its rear that led to a screened-in porch.

One day, the story goes, Father Groff had to leave the study hall for more than a minute or two. How the fellows assigned to the hall knew that he would be gone that long is included in the long list entitled, "The Things Students Know That Teachers Don't Know That They Know." While Father Groff was gone, the boys exited, one and all, to the porch and closed the door behind them. On his return, Father Groff found the study hall empty.

Anyone putting himself or herself in the shoes of this rookie teacher can imagine the combination of wonderment and fear that must have swept over him. So Father Groff did what anyone would do—he went looking for the AWOL seventy-five. Not quickly finding them, he must have swallowed hard before he sought help. The tale states that Father Tribou was called in, and they both returned to the study hall—now re-populated with all its original inhabitants. No doubt an explanation about the porch soon followed.

*****

Behind his back we called Father Frederick Zarilli "Zeke." It was a nickname that always seemed apt to me—it was friendly, as he was. Father Zarilli was one of many CHS priests who participated in the shuttle service to get us to our out-of-town basketball games. Maybe this procedure was set up to save the school money—no bus need be rented—maybe the priests who took us in groups of four and five just liked going to Morrilton and other spots to see us play.

With Father Zarilli driving, we always had to be on the alert. He informed us every time we drove that he was color-blind. He could always tell whether an oncoming traffic light was lit on the top or the bottom by its glow. The problem was that some towns, like Morrilton, had the red light on the bottom and the green on top. I had then and have now no idea how this departure from the norm ever came into being, but as soon as we began to drive through a small town, all of us passengers focused on just one thing as Father Z would say, "OK, boys, tell me what you see."

It was as if the duty could not be trusted to one boy alone. We all leaned forward to ascertain the position of the red and the green, simultaneously alerting him to color, position, etc. It was a group effort that saw us safely through many a town. How he got along without us when driving through a strange town I'll never know.

*****

Father Zarilli was the teacher on duty in the library at the old school when Lee Rogers whispered that he knew the "most beautiful word in English." The priest on duty was supposed to be sure that silence reigned in the library—no talking or goofing off allowed.

"So, what's the most beautiful word?" I obliged, anticipating the punch line.

"Rot," said Lee.

It struck me as mildly funny—at first. Then, given the circumstances, where even a slight guffaw might draw a disapproving glance from Father Z, it became funnier. I was trying my best to restrain myself, even to the point of bending over in my chair and hiding behind the table so that the priest, who was on the balcony where he could observe from above, might not see me. Other students present noted my contorted, shaking body and found it amusing. They began to titter. I was only spurred on by their laughs, realizing that they hadn't a clue as to what was funny. Nearly crying out in pain from the repressed laughter, I finally began chortling aloud, and others joined me. As the hilarity grew, Father Zarilli, who had been absorbed in a book until the out-loud laughs began, leaned over the edge of the balcony to assess the situation. As he did, the raucous laughter overtook the library—and him as well, and it came to pass that we all were enjoying a belly laugh of the first rank, all because of "rot."

*****

Lunchtime at the old school was perhaps thirty minutes long, time enough after a quick sandwich to spend some outside. The grounds around the school included a large, open expanse of clay that seemed incapable of growing any grass. The freshman football team practiced there after school, though it wasn't as large as a full-sized football field.

One lunchtime diversion was "Kill the Man with the Ball," a spirited game that for whatever reason the authorities never saw fit to ban, despite more than a few injuries and fights that it spawned. The game was simple: Someone got a football and ran with it wherever he wished on the concrete-like clay, until he was tackled. He then struggled to his feet and either gave the ball to a particular participant who, in turn, ran for his life, or the ball would be tossed in the air for anyone to catch and take off.

It happened one day that a thrown ball bounced into Father Zarilli's hands. He was apparently the day's designated monitor of the madness. Much to my amazement (I was no fan of "Kill" except as an observer) I saw Father Zarilli begin to run with the ball. The herd that had chased down the toss that he fielded backed away momentarily from the sight of a priest on the run. I don't know if Father Z said something challenging to them or if the pack mentality overcame the usual deference to a priest, but suddenly the chase was on! Father Zarilli wasn't exactly well suited to outrunning a pride of teenagers, given his age and the fact that he was wearing a cassock, that priestly garb that extended, skirt-like, to his ankles.

Amazing was the sight of my Latin teacher, slightly rotund and surely forty-ish, flying past the would-be tacklers, who were in full-throated cry by now. Not only that, Father Zarilli shed some would-be tacklers as if they were raindrops on cement. He circled the whole field, and the pursuers, seeing his speed and power, gave up. Father Zarilli suddenly stopped within a few feet of me, a big grin on his face. He didn't even seem winded. He tossed the ball to one of the many he had vanquished and said, "I think I lost my watch." A quick hunt by what had been the frustrated posse shortly turned it up. Had I not been so awestruck by the whole pursuit and the fact that a priest was involved, I'm sure I would have given Father Zarilli what was the compliment of the times: "Way to be, Zeke!"

*****

Father (now Monsignor) Gaston Hebert began his CHS career when I was a student there, and he was still on the faculty when I began as a teacher. He was then the head of the English department and was kind enough to talk to me prior to my first day as a teacher. He was most encouraging and assured me that he thought I would do a fine job as a teacher. Obviously he had little on which to base his rosy prediction, but I've always been grateful to him for it, nonetheless.

One thing Father Hebert especially wanted me to do was to utilize our closed-circuit TV station, which had recently been installed. Catholic High hasn't often been in the vanguard of technological change (was it 2002 when we got e-mail?), but the TV studio was a gift of Harry Hastings, a local businessman, and so into the gift horse's mouth CHS did not want to seem to be looking.

Father Hebert was so lenient that he allowed me to teach a grammar program adopting the persona of football coach Jacques E. Strapp. So I donned a ball cap and hung a whistle around my neck and shouted at my nouns, verbs, and all the rest of my troops, drawing out "plays" on a blackboard as to where they should be if success was to be ours. As I said, Father Hebert was very tolerant.

*****

Father Hebert had perhaps the oddest course at Catholic High. It was called Speech—not unusual on the face of it. The oddness consisted in all the things that Father Hebert thought of for his class to learn besides giving persuasive or expository speeches. He taught them bridge. He taught them how to operate a washer and dryer. He taught them to cook. He taught them table manners. What graduate of what was often labeled a "male chauvinist" school would not have benefitted from such a course!

*****

Father Bernard DeBosier was one of CHS's truly memorable characters. He was first brought to my new-kid-on-the-block attention as a fellow faculty member when Father Tribou was outlining my duties as the sophomore English teacher. He stated that I would be teaching both literature and grammar. He mentioned in passing that Father D, who instructed juniors and seniors, taught no grammar—just American and British Literature.

"Why doesn't he teach grammar? " I nosily if innocently asked. Father Tribou curtly said, "I haven't asked." It didn't occur to me that the reason Father Tribou hadn't asked was because he didn't want to ruffle Father D's feathers. This seemed like an issue that was easily made comprehensible. "Do you want me to ask him?" I offered. Father Tribou looked over his glasses and responded dryly, "I'd like to sell tickets to that."

Slow as I was to grasp some things about my new job, I quickly gathered that Father DeBosier was not someone with whom one should trifle—not even Father Tribou. It wasn't that Father D was ill-tempered, but it's fair to say that many of us, teachers and students alike, sensed that beneath his jolly surface lurked something that one didn't want to be responsible for unleashing.

*****

I suspect every boy who had "Bernie," as Father DeBosier was affectionately known to his students, would vouch for the fact that he could muster some seemingly volcanic outrage when students crossed him. But these outbursts had the element of theater about them. "Boy, I'm going to tear off that ignorant head of yours and roll it down the hall like a bowling ball!" was the kind of dramatic line that he could deliver. But did his students fear him as a result? I think not. That was just Father DeBosier being Father DeBosier. While few took these moments of apparent rage seriously, I think we all suspected that they just might have a real component hiding behind the histrionics, so one didn't push him too far.

*****

Father DeBosier was a fluent, mellifluous speaker of the English language. It offended him to hear it mangled, so when one of his students made an especially egregious error, Father D invoked a power even higher than himself in his condemnation: "Boy, you are fracturing the King's English!"

One can only guess at the dismay Father D must have felt in terms of how far he had to go to succeed with that particular student after hearing his response: "I don't care about no King!"

*****

No one who attended CHS during Father DeBosier's time would have failed to hear him say, "I'm not just standing out here waving my arms like the village idiot!" He bellowed out that sentence many times as the student body, assembled in the gym, was practicing singing for an upcoming Mass. Father D led the practices, and he invariably reminded all in attendance, with the "idiot" declaration, that they should be watching him for direction. In that era, singing practice was held at the end of the day, during what was called Activity Period. Father D invariably lamented the lack of volume produced by the 700 or so "singers" present. Then he figured out a way to get the students to produce the volume he desired.

No doubt this was in cahoots with Father Tribou, but it was a stunningly simple plan that always worked. At some point Father DeBosier would say, "Boys, if we have to stay after school to get you to sing as loud as you can, that's what we'll do. However, if you will give me what I want in the way of volume, I am authorized to dismiss you early." Result? Rafters were rattled, the loudness problem was solved—and school was out!

*****

Father Raymond Rossi was a Catholic High alumnus who returned to teach at his alma mater (I must be sure to get all Latinate words exactly right, since Latin was Father Rossi's area of expertise). He was, in his student days, a Rocket footballer who later was team chaplain after his assignment to CHS.

Father Rossi was passionate about Latin, and he did his utmost to pass on that fervor, regardless of the resistance of twentieth-century students, many of whom ascribed to the old saw, "Latin is a deadly language, that is plain to see. First it killed the Romans, and now it's killing me!" He taught at a crescendo level, his voice pounding up against and penetrating even the most unwilling-to-hear. He could be heard from several classrooms away when doors were open. One day I crossed paths with a student just after school was out, and he looked slightly dazed, perhaps a bit disoriented. I inquired about his condition. "I just got through with Father Rossi's class, and he taught with both the door and the windows closed. I'm shell-shocked!"

Stories are legion about Father Rossi's outbursts of enthusiasm. Many claim to have seen this incident: Agitated by widespread scholastic ineptitude, concerning perhaps, students' inability to grasp the dative of possession or the first active periphrastic conjugation, Father Rossi threw his glasses down on his desk, located near the window, at such an angle that they caromed off the desktop and exited the window. I never confirmed that with him, but there are those who swear it was so.

*****

It was a standing joke among Father Rossi's fellow faculty members that we needn't read Father Tribou's faculty bulletin board notices each morning. If we just waited until Father Rossi arrived in the faculty lounge to do his own reading, we could just listen in. As previously noted, Father Rossi had a powerful voice, and even reading the announcements to himself was enough volume to inform the others present. Not only that, but one could get Father Rossi's editorial comments on the events of the day. "Fire drill at fourth period. Dang! That's going to cut down on my test time!" or "Pep rally at the end of the day. Good thing we don't have to try to teach them after that's over." He was our clarion (from the Latin *clarus*, clear).

*****

Known throughout most of his Catholic High career as "Father Fred," Father (now Monsignor) Lawrence Frederick was also a Catholic High grad who came back to teach. As of this writing, he is in his forty-first year at CHS, having taught Religion, Physics, and Mechanical Drawing to thousands. He has also done double-duty for more than a decade by teaching Religion and Physics at Mt. St. Mary's as well.

Like Father Rossi, Father Fred has a voice that resembles the blast of a trumpet, the kind that brought Jericho's walls tumbling down. It's not often that he employs this instrument with its full impact (perhaps his knowledge of physics leads him to prudent use in the presence of things that might fall or crumble). But there are times when the voice gets its full volume effect involuntarily: when Fr. Frederick laughs. You may have heard some potent laughter in your time, but we'd match You-know-who with anybody for sheer decibel power. It's infectious, like many things about the man, and it is a force of nature one cannot ignore.

At Catholic High we have altered the cliché, and thus we say, "It <u>does</u> take a Rocket scientist" because Father Fred is indeed that: a CHS alumnus who did become a scientist—in fact, a N.A.S.A. engineer involved in some space-age stuff prior to becoming a priest. And he knows a lot! I give you, for example his scholarly explanation to me as to how radio works: "It's magic!" With incisive explications such as that, who could fail to learn from such a

The '58 faculty included Mr. Mike Malham, Fr. John Doyle, Fr. George Tribou, Fr. Frederick Zarilli, Fr. Francis Colavechio, Fr. William Galvin, Fr. Leo Riedmuller, Fr. Reuben Groff, Fr. Milton Lange, Mr. Jim Collier—absent was Fr. John O'Donnell.

teacher? Father Fred also liked to agitate what little grey matter I have that attempts to understand science by telling me how a clothes drier works: "The water doesn't come out of the clothes; the clothes come out of the water." The gleam he gets in his eyes when he makes such pronouncements gives indication that one is in the company of a man who could bedazzle a student with very little effort—a gifted teacher.

*****

As of 2009, Father Frederick is the sole priest on a faculty that once had thirteen priests during my tenure as a teacher. He is the Rector of Catholic High School, the religious head of our scholastic community. What the future holds for our school in the way of priestly presence is unknown. Should it happen, as it has happened elsewhere, that a priest in residence is not an everyday fact about our school, and should Monsignor Lawrence Frederick be the last of his line, then the end of the tradition will have ended with a bang, not a whimper. I am eager to state my opinion, based on forty-four years of experience, that the boys of Catholic High School who have known him have been fortunate for his example of dedication to his vocation. Words like *faithful* and *honest* and *holy* come to my mind to describe Lawrence A. Frederick, a kid who, at St. Patrick's in North Little Rock and then at CHS, came to an understanding of what God called him to be. I am proud to call him "Father" and "friend."

*****

Richard Althoff was an alumnus who taught mathematics. That's the kind of sentence that, on the one hand, sums up a person, and on the other, doesn't begin to touch his reality. His all-too-short life was spent bringing sunshine into the lives of others. I haven't known a person warmer or more engaging. He was smart, funny, humble, athletic, loyal, and almost too good to be true.

Richard rose from a huge Althoff family, and his brothers also were CHS grads. It was a blessing to Catholic High to have so many fine young men from just one family who contributed to the common weal of our school. If I may generalize about the Althoff sons, I will say that they share a common trait, surely due to their parents' influence: They are genuine. This appealing characteristic shone brightly in Richard. He was what he was—an unpretentious person whose goodness was a magnet for others, students and teachers alike.

Most of the time outside of school hours that I spent with Richard was on a golf course. Approximately thirty years ago, he, Don Lawson, David Westmoreland, and I began to play nine holes almost every Friday after school at Rebsamen Golf Course. When Steve Wells joined the faculty, he became a fixture as well. Other teachers joined the group—some like Dick Heien, for many years, while others played only a year or two and then either decided to find a higher class group with whom to hang out or moved on from CHS.

As Richard was in the vanguard of introducing some new technology to CHS called computers, he also managed to use them to keep track of each player's stroke average and handicap. We thought this was a math mystery brought to life, as each Monday he had a printout ready with all the previous Friday's numbers crunched, arranged, and evoking our awe.

I haven't known many ambidextrous people in my lifetime, but Richard was one of them, though he was primarily a right-hander. As such, Richard exhibited another Althoff family characteristic: the ability to hit a golf ball an extraordinarily long way. Most of the Althoff brothers apparently shared a misspent youth caddying and playing lots of rounds at the now defunct North Hills Country Club, but their experience showed in their play. One day Richard's ability to wallop the ball did, however, put him in a ticklish position with regard to the Little Rock police.

What we always called "the short nine" at Rebsamen used to have one par-five hole, not especially long by most course standards. It might have been about 500 yards long, and it wasn't often that any in our group could get to the green in two shots—except Richard. As we approached the hole during a round, we saw a police car parked very near the green. Having seen that, we then spied two policemen off to the side of the fairway, peering in the direction of the Arkansas River, which ran parallel to the hole. They were looking at a Jeep that someone had run out onto a sandbar when the water level was low, and which now was stranded after a rise in the water.

The police car was so near the green that no one other than Richard was likely to hit it on the second shot. But he was an accurate striker of the ball, so he went for the green. When Richard took his mighty swing and then said, "Uh oh!" we expected the worst. Richard had this one time pulled his shot. Speaking of "shot," that is what the ball caroming off the police car sounded like. Richard manfully headed in the direction of the two policemen, who had undoubtedly heard the ball hit. As he went to apologize and see what needed to be done to rectify the situation, he was in a spot none of us envied. As he turned away from the police after speaking to them and began to walk toward us, his big, beaming smile told us that all was well. "Don't worry about it," was what he told us they said. I wouldn't be surprised if their forgiving response was due to Richard's sincerity and apparent desire to set things right.

*****

Richard's all-too-early death from cancer took a loving husband, father, and friend, as well as an excellent teacher. He was a man I admired deeply and whose company I cherished. He was capable of laughing at himself, as he did when he announced at a Parent Teacher Meeting that he and fellow Driver's Education instructor Bob Palazzi would be late starting the course that summer because, as he put it, "Bob and I are getting married." His pause that followed gave the assembled hundreds of parents time to digest the remark and then begin to laugh heartily, as did Richard when he realized what he had said. His sense of humor was matched by his sense of integrity, and he was not only a model for his students but his colleagues on the faculty as well.

*****

A year after Richard's death began the tradition of playing the Richard Althoff Memorial Golf Tournament at the beginning of Spring Break each year. The tournament has always concluded with a gathering at either a park or restaurant where those of us who knew Richard tell the faculty newcomers who he was and why we honor his memory each year. Recently Dennis and Bob Althoff, two of his brothers, have joined us, excellent players both, and it seems fitting that almost every year that they play, the plaque that hangs in the faculty room with the names of each year's winners on it has another "Althoff" added to it. We still miss him.

*****

Father William Galvin was principal when I was a student. A short, barrel-chested fellow, Father Galvin was, in the words of a student who had given some thought to it, "…like the CEO of Catholic High—a strong presence but one who delegated well." It was Father Galvin who oversaw the efforts to raise the money to build the new Catholic High. Eventually succeeded by Father Tribou, Monsignor Galvin went on to run a large parish—surely in the efficient way he did CHS.

When I was a senior, I heard that part of our Religion course for the year was to be a six-week course with Father Galvin—on the subject of marriage. I wasn't the only one who found exciting the prospect of getting an inside glimpse into this *terra incognita*.

Tom Larrison, a classmate, was eager to find out from the start about what we all surely thought was the most important aspect of marriage. Tom asked Father Galvin directly, "Father, before a guy gets married does the priest give him a book?" Father Galvin was puzzled: "A book? What kind of book?" My guess is that Tom hoped no explanation was necessary, but he soldiered on: "You know, a book that tells you what to *do*?" Father Galvin didn't yet seem to know what "book" Tom was talking about, but we knew what he meant! Father Galvin was still perplexed, but then it dawned on him what Tom (and we) wanted to learn about. "No, Tom, the priest doesn't give you a book. You can ask your father about what you need to know." Hoping as Tom possibly was that such heart-to-heart talks with our fathers wouldn't have been necessary, I'm sure we shared his disappointment about the lack of an instruction manual.

As it turned out, Father Galvin's class on marriage was about very practical things like budgets and rearing children. In other words, it wasn't as stimulating as we'd hoped it would be. One Friday afternoon we were taking turns reading from our text. I blame the rigors of the week, the time of day, and the heat of the classroom for what happened next. Father Galvin called on me to read. The problem was I was nearly asleep. In retrospect, I think he knew this. The sound of my name startled me. I was discombobulated, having no idea where in the text we were. An alert and helpful classmate pointed clearly in his book to the spot where the reading should begin. And so I groggily began to read. My fog hadn't lifted entirely, and I obviously mispronounced a word. I say "obviously" because I heard Father Galvin correcting me. I'm not exactly sure what I said in response, but I think it must have been the 1961 version of "whatever." Nowadays, that word has the power to inflame agitation in the person (an adult) to whom it is directed (by an adolescent), so indifferent to that person's concerns is the user of that term.

Whatever I said had that same effect on Father Galvin. He called on another person to read. I gratefully sat down, looking to resume my siesta. But I then heard his voice again. "Moran, take your books, leave the room, and stand out in the hall until the period ends." I was shocked, but I scrambled to follow the orders, so curtly and in such a no-nonsense tone were they given. When the bell rang to end the class, and the week, I wandered off, a bit puzzled by Father Galvin's reaction. Classmates I saw after school thought the situation odd as well, but I didn't make much of it, not until the following Monday when I walked into his class and sat down.

As class began, Father Galvin asked a student to hand out a sheet of paper to everyone "...except to Moran. Moran, leave the room, stand in the hall, and see me after school today." As I rose to go, I was beyond shock. This was baffling. For the remainder of the class I stood outside the classroom as before, not knowing what was going on. At lunch my classmates were as clueless as I. "Well, I guess you'll find out after school today," one opined. And I did. I sought out Father Galvin in his office. He looked at me squarely, as was his wont, and said, "What have you to say for yourself?" "I don't know what to say." He paused, perhaps wondering if I was as dumb as I sounded. "How about 'I'm sorry'?"

Had my parents known then or ever (I'm sure I never told them this story) that they had brought up a son so dense that he would not know when an apology was called for, I'm sure they would have been embarrassed. I know I was. The simple act of asking for forgiveness for boorish behavior hadn't occurred to me. I immediately did say I was sorry—and meant it. Father Galvin never later gave me cause to think, by anything that he said or did, that his acceptance of my apology was anything but genuine. I regretted everything about the situation, and never dreamed that I would someday be involved in one much like it—but this time as a teacher.

In the spring of 2008, my last year, a senior sitting in the last seat of a row did something untoward that caused me to correct him. I was near his desk at the time and so the correction wasn't very public. Whatever anti-social behavior he was exhibiting, it ended. Within a few minutes, however, he was talking to the student next to him. My ego doesn't allow for such, so I glared at him—again, a somewhat low-profile reproof. He stopped talking. This lad, ordinarily a solid citizen in my class, had one more deviation from the norm to exercise—I think he wasn't on the same page as the rest of us. At any rate, it was one time too many for me. And so, on that Friday afternoon, I said, "Take your books and leave. Stand outside for the remainder of the class." It was the last period of the day for me to teach, so when the bell sounded to end the period, he headed off for his next class and I was off to the golf course to pay the greens fees for my fellow teachers who would be along soon. In other words, I wasn't thinking of the boy I tossed. That didn't come to me until the following Monday, just before the period began when I was to teach that student.

It was then that I thought of Father Galvin, and realized that, like him, I thought I was owed an apology. I wondered how the 2008 version of this story would play out. As the boy in question walked into my room, I told him, to his surprise, to turn around and go into the hall and wait for me. The other students filed in; I read from the gospel of Mathew, took the roll, filled out an absentee slip, and took it to the door to place it in a small slot on the hall-side of the door.

My expellee stood in the hall, looking abject. I wondered how much of my experience he was about to repeat. "Have you anything to say to me?" I said, channeling Father Galvin. "Mr. Moran, I'm really sorry and promise not to act that way again," he said earnestly. As I ushered him back into the classroom, I recognized that a boy in 2008 was smarter and better mannered than one in 1961.

*****

Mrs. Woody Butler was the mother of my CHS basketball teammate, Woody Butler, Jr. As a faculty member I knew her in another context: Kathryn Butler headed the Catholic High cafeteria for twenty years. She was a no-nonsense boss of the cafeteria, and the food was generally excellent. Many who partook of Mrs. Butler's fare can recount favorites: Frito pie, mouth-watering dinner rolls made from scratch the morning they were served, a Thanksgiving meal as good (or better?) than one would get at home, and the interestingly paired duet of pizza and corn. She was affectionately known as "Ma" Butler to a generation of CHS boys.

My colleague Steve Wells was doing lunch patrol duty when a disgruntled student approached him. "Mr. Wells, where do I go to get my money back?" Steve asked him what the problem was, and the boy showed him a hair lying atop a piece of meatloaf that he had just purchased from the cafeteria. Steve knew Mrs. Butler probably wouldn't take kindly to an indignant student commenting negatively about the food, but he figured the lad had to find that out for himself, so he directed him to where Mrs. Butler was working in the kitchen and returned to his post. Steve soon heard raised voices coming from the kitchen and decided he'd better investigate.

Mrs. Butler had every cafeteria employee lined up in front of the complainant. Each employee was not only wearing an all-encompassing hair net, but each was a brunette (as was she). As Mrs. Butler held up the long, blonde hair that had sparked the lad's outrage, she demanded of hapless boy, "So tell me, where did the hair come from?" The befuddled student's reply is not recorded, though were I in his situation, I'm sure abject groveling would have ensued.

*****

When I thought about Kathryn Butler's service to CHS, I ventured into the world of mathematics to get some sense of the magnitude of her contribution. See if you think I've done my arithmetic correctly: 20 years of serving lunch times 180 days per year equals 3,600 days. If one inserts a conservative estimate of 400 boys a day eating lunch served by Mrs. B, one gets a total of 1,440,000. Kathryn Butler fed Catholic High boys almost one-and-a-half million meals. I join the chorus of lads who shouted appreciatively from the cafeteria to the kitchen at the end of a really tasty meal, "Good lunch, Ma!"

*****

Susan Gray, who for many years excelled as teacher of Spanish and French, told me of this improbable exchange:

Questioner: "Where do you work?"

Susan Gray: "I teach at Catholic High School."

Questioner: "You mean Mt. St. Mary's, don't you?"

As astonishing as that bit of give-and-take is, I was further astounded when Bitsi Bonner, herself a skilled teacher at CHS in both the Speech and English departments, told me she, too, had been asked the same doubting question when she told someone she worked at CHS. To think that people believe that intelligent women with college degrees must be confused about their place of employment signals a disconnect between the role of women at CHS and some outsiders' assumptions about what that role must be.

So my lesson today is that CHS is not an all-male enclave. For those who are new to the notion that women play a vital role at CHS, I can inform them that there was a woman on the faculty at CHS at least as far back as the 1940's. It would be hard to overestimate the contributions that women teachers have made at Catholic High, and most any graduate since the late 1960's has likely had several women instructors.

It occurred to me to try to identify all our unsung heroines, both teachers and staff, who have had a positive impact on Catholic High boys, but a dreadful thought kept intruding: What if I leave someone out? My recollection isn't potent enough to include all. I decided to try at least to name all those who gave a decade or more of their lives to CHS. Even at that, I'll probably fail. So I apologize in advance to those whom I've neglected to name and offer as some consolation lines taken from Robert Bolt's *A Man for All Seasons*; they occur as Thomas More is trying to influence Richard Rich's career choice:

MORE Why not be a teacher? You'd be a fine teacher. Perhaps even a great one.

RICH And if I was, who would know it?

MORE You, your pupils, your friends, God. Not a bad public, that.

Acknowledging that my memory isn't potent enough to identify every woman who did and does act in a vital role at CHS, I trust that no one will gainsay me if I salute the woman who taught more years at CHS than any other. She was the foundation upon which countless Catholic High boys' successful careers were based. She taught English so well to ninth graders that subsequent English classes were facilitated by the fine start that she provided. She sponsored the CHS newspaper for many years, and even in retirement she shows up regularly to tutor students who will certainly be fortunate, as have thousands of others, for having had Ms. Jo Schneider as their teacher.

Having announced that I would try to identify those women who have taught or served on the staff at CHS for at least ten years, I plead at the outset that my historical research is probably flawed, and I fear that I shall be ruing my lapses "somewhere ages and ages hence," but I shall try anyway.

The aforementioned duo of Susan Gray and Bitsi Bonner are indeed in the group, as are Norma Martine and Pam Hunter, excellent math teachers both; Shelby Schichtl taught typing to thousands; Jackie Thomas is an expert

Biology instructor; Beverly Billingsley achieved her decade of service as talented teacher of English and a faithful Library Mom after her retirement; Sylvia Chudy was a Father Tribou favorite for running a tight ship in the library; Gretchen Gowen is a multi-talented English teacher; Bernice Ritter Elias remarkably could and did teach both Biology and English. Staff members who served a decade or more include Marie Woeltje, who was both secretary and bookkeeper; Barbara Pierce, who has skillfully kept track of increasingly complex financial matters; Eleanor Hannah and Joan Finnegan, whose work proved the widespread belief that secretaries are the real heads of any school.

Not to emphasize only the fairer sex, I honor the work of the men not previously or eventually discussed in detail, who also gave Catholic High at least ten years of their lives during my time as a teacher: Paul Stiedle taught Calculus to many who later found the college version "a snap"; Roy Davis led the football Rockets to two state championships and is a computer guru to boot; Ronny Tollett, who introduced his fellow faculty members to the powers of the overhead projector, was both biology teacher and basketball coach; Paul Spencer figured out how to elucidate social studies to both freshmen and seniors; Jerry Reasor was our high-tech fellow, teaching keyboarding and computer programming; Tim Ezzi has taught health and ended the 78-year basketball championship drought; Dick Heien has taught, coached, and counseled with great success; the priestly brothers Oswald, John and Richard, were skilled in science and math; speaking of science, Jim Edge is and has been the Chemistry mainstay for more than a quarter century; Tim Glancy also taught science and coached several sports at his alma mater; John Hall, before he went to his everyday job, came to teach Religion; Bob Palazzi taught math and introduced both psychology and driver education; Carl Imhauser was our head of maintenance for many years; Jack Hennelley made an indelible mark upon the JROTC department and trained the first CHS national championship physical fitness team; Steve Wells, though prominently mentioned, must be noted for the double distinction of teaching brilliantly and leading the physical fitness team to its second national championship; Jack Pritchett has taught music and led the CHS band to its reputation as one of the state's best; Doug Pilcher taught history and was head football coach; Paul Shaffer guided the JROTC program to high achievement; Sherrill Baker also proved to be invaluable to the JROTC; "Magist" means to any Latin student his memorable teacher, Tom Handloser; Cody McDaniel has led our Fed Challenge team to a championship—and golf teams as well; Tommy Coy sparked many a math mind; Dan Smith diligently taught math and coached as well; Don Lawson was the social studies anchor for a quarter-century; Steve Straessle continues to shine as both teacher and principal.

I pray I have recalled all whom I set out to remember.

*****

Among my assorted memories of Catholic High are bits and pieces of recollections about various faculty and staff members I have known. These are only fragments of people's lives. The stories don't begin to take in the totality of the people who figure in them. Some of these reflections do concern a

Mr. Richard Althoff set the standard for teachers in terms of devotion to his students and his skill in teaching.

common assumption about CHS that I hope to disprove: that teaching here

is easy because all the boys are well mannered and respectful. The fact is,

despite the truth that we have many such fine lads on our rolls, we also have

many who are not that way—or, at least, are not at first. Catholic High has

reputation as a no-nonsense school that insists on disciplined behavior from

its students. And to the extent that it is such a school, it is so as the result of great effort on the part of the administration, faculty and students. It isn't a given. It doesn't come about except through persistent effort.

*****

One teacher, new to the teaching profession and thus to CHS, quit within the first month. She taught sophomores biology and apparently found the tenth-graders more than she bargained for. The grapevine communicated to CHS that she soon got a job at a local medical laboratory, a fitting spot for a biology major, one would suppose. When we heard further in what work she was engaged, which was an analysis of rodent feces, we could only agree with the wag who summed it up: "She preferred rat dung to Catholic High sophomores."

*****

Another instructor, a man in perhaps his late twenties, was let go by Father Tribou just as the Christmas holidays were about to start, a traumatic event for both the young fellow and the school, given the unfortunate timing. No doubt Father T was pained mightily by the onerous duty. One assumes he had no choice, however, when rumors that the teacher was making some extra cash after hours turned out to be confirmed. One can't imagine our principal hanging on to someone who was a CHS teacher by day and an exotic dancer by night.

*****

When news of what's going on at school reaches the ears of faculty members, it can be very old hat to the students. So when I first heard that a new biology teacher, a fellow in his twenties with some prior experience in teaching, was having trouble controlling his students, it had probably been a fact for some time. It can take a while for a new teacher to learn to control the boys. I have seen men who were six-four and carried 250 pounds who could not manage it, and women who were little more than five feet tall and weighed barely 100 pounds who could. It has to do with an aspect of character that is hard to define, but it seems to boil down to a determination not to fail. The young instructor in question was possibly lacking that quality.

One day I substituted for the teacher whose classroom was next door to the biology teacher's. I gave no thought to his nearby presence for a few minutes. The fellows I was sitting with were quietly studying. Then the volume from the room next door began to rise. It wasn't like a shout at a football game; it was like someone slowly turning up the volume on a radio. It eventually became a loud roar. I looked at the boys with whom I was sitting, and they seemed to notice it very little. The sound increased, and then I heard someone shouting, "Shut up! Shut up!" Well, at least the new teacher was battling. Then I heard the same voice say again, "Shut up! Let him teach!" It was a student yelling at his mates to quiet down. The volume did decrease a little, but the uproar was audible off and on throughout the rest of the period. As the bell rang and the students whom I was watching were filing out, I must have had a horrified or astounded look on my face. Responding to that, one of the exiting fellows stopped and said matter-of-factly, "It happens every day." Despite Father Tribou's best efforts to help the young teacher get to that "I-won't-be-deterred" attitude, he never did, and his career at CHS concluded that year.

*****

A young, single woman interviewed with Father Tribou in the spring for an opening that was coming up in the fall. When the first day of school arrived four or five months later, our opening-day assembly in the gym featured, as it always did, Father T's introduction of new teachers. When he introduced this particular young woman, he announced that she was "Mrs." So-and-so and had been married just a month before. It was only then that I noticed, as perhaps hundreds of students did, that she was evidently pregnant.

The muffled faculty-room conversations after school that day centered on two questions: When is the baby due? Does Father Tribou know? Female faculty members were given their due as to being the best diviners of both answers. Their verdict was twofold: "Any day now" and "No," especially given his introduction of her to the boys. After further discussion, one of the women volunteered or was out of the room when the vote was taken, and she was commissioned to alert Father T to the situation. The upshot was that the women were right on both counts: It was to be soon, and he hadn't known. Not many weeks later she gave birth. I have no idea of the details worked out between her and Father T, but she didn't return to CHS to teach.

So Father Tribou was in a tough spot. He had to find a replacement a month or so into the school year. An alumnus happened to drop by during this time, and Father T asked him in what discipline was his college degree. It just so happened to be in exactly the subject that the woman taught. Father T begged him to come on board until he could find a full-time teacher—substituting for "perhaps a few weeks." And that is how, twenty-five years ago, Mr. Steve Wells got a temporary job at his alma mater. He is still waiting for the full-time replacement to show up.

*****

A highly qualified man with multiple degrees who was in his mid-forties was hired by Father Tribou to teach social studies. Before his first (and last) year was done, his name became known far beyond the limits of the classes he taught. One factor that added to his fame was the ingenuity of the members of those very classes. They were remarkable for the variety of deviations from the norm that they could imagine.

"Quit your skylarkin'!" was this man's unique battle-cry in opposition to any and all who were acting outside the bounds of proper behavior. He used the mantra on occasions too numerous to count. Skylarkin' was exemplified by his students silently scooting their desks in his direction as, at his desk, he read the text non-stop. It was only when all thirty of them were within ten feet of him that he realized their proximity. That evoked the loud accusation that skylarkin' was in progress.

The same could be said for the class's ability to blame the innocent for their misdeeds. When untoward behavior erupted, usually in the form of something shouted or said, this teacher was seldom able to pinpoint the perpetrator. He then would unwisely inquire, "Who did it?" One of the members of this class was noted for his habitual taciturnity. He was known to utter as few words as possible—as if he had taken a vow of silence. It was he, of course, whom the others immediately accused of the sound, regardless of whether it came from the part of the room where he was seated. Taking the class's word for it, the teacher would remind the alleged perpetrator about the need to avoid behaviors associated with the skylark and send him to the office.

Father Tribou, who knew of the lad's closed-mouth tendencies, was surprised when he first saw the boy sitting in the office with a hangdog look, and he couldn't believe his ears when the lad told him he'd been sent there by Mr. So-and-so for misbehavior. After a few more of the boy's enforced visits to the principal on succeeding days, Father T had to break the news to the teacher that the fellow he considered a trouble-maker had the conversational tendencies of a cloistered monk, and that the teacher should do better job of nabbing his miscreants.

One of the features of this teacher's class was "extra credit." This was a process by which students could turn in class-related work that went beyond the bounds of normal assignments. Or at least that was the theory behind extra credit. Someone tested out a theory about extra credit that proved true: The teacher paid no mind to the content of the work; he just counted how many pages were turned in. Once that information entered the public domain, on the day near the end of each nine weeks when extra credit was due, the teacher's desk was piled high with paper, some of it that students had left over from previous years, such as sophomore biology notes. Students who saw the piles of paper on the teacher's desk invariably resorted to words like *heaps*, *mounds*, and *mountains* to describe them.

Perhaps the crowning event in this man's story was his giving an A on a term paper written by the twelve-year-old sister of a D student, and returning an F to the lad who would be identified as valedictorian at the following year's graduation. There was no logic to explain his academic conclusions, and the grades were the talk of the school. Somehow Father Tribou intervened to rectify the injustice.

When it came time to fire the fellow, Father T's job was made easier by the man's breezily entering his office and immediately quoting from John Donne's famous *Meditation 17*: "Never send to know for whom the bell tolls, it tolls for thee." Such a dramatic valedictory deserves a slightly altered Shakespearian response: "Nothing in his career became him like the leaving of it."

*****

Mrs. Robert Schichtl (known to her sister and brother teachers as Shelby) was enduring on a daily basis a trial of which I was unaware until one day when I was asked to substitute for her. Over the years Shelby taught typing to a legion of CHS boys, and I never realized the fortitude and resolve it took to face them throughout what was a five-classes-a-day schedule. As I was a last-minute replacement, Father Tribou advised me to tell the boys just to continue with their typing practice from their workbooks. I would guess that Shelby's typing room had about twenty-five typewriters— old-style manual types, which required a firm stroke to produce even a single letter.

So I began the class with the usual prayer and then pointed out the obvious, that I wasn't Mrs. Schichtl, and told the boys to get to work with their typing lessons. The boys responded well, sitting down, rolling pieces of paper into their machines, and then they began. The clatter, the ricocheting sound, the staccato pounding startled me so much that I felt myself lurch backward in the chair into which I had just sat.

The boys were absolutely indifferent to the wall of sound they were creating. I had planned to do some grading while watching over the typing class, but I found the sound so distracting that I accomplished little in the fifty minutes I was there. But the boys appeared to get a lot done as they typed away at a frantic pace. I did some walking about the room to be sure that they weren't just hitting the same keys over and over, and what I saw was the kind of desired product in a typing class, with words and phrases repeated time and again to further one's skill. When she returned the next day, I told Shelby of my admiration for her ability to put up with the pounding, but she acted as if it were no great accomplishment. It was to me.

*****

Mr. James Perry was the custodian at Catholic High for many years. He was not only an excellent worker but also a beloved figure. I don't know how Mr. Perry could smile so often at the very boys who made his life difficult when they thoughtlessly created messes of one kind or another, but he did. From time to time he would regale the students with his harmonica-playing, a treat that the boys always vigorously applauded. He rarely had a complaint to utter about teen-aged lack of order. It's fair to say that he took justifiable pride in the look of the school because he was primarily responsible for it. When he finished swirling the heavy buffer down a hall he had just waxed, Mr. Perry had brought back the surface shine it had when the school was new. Father Tribou, an especially good steward of the building and grounds, would walk about the school with a small tape recorder in hand and make verbal notes of what needed tending to. Mr. Perry was his right-hand man in these matters. It was he who obliterated an offending graffito that might pop up somewhere, or mop up something that had marred the beauty of his floors.

I remember seeing Mr. Perry plant some small trees in front of the classroom wing that faces the Father Frederick Science Building, long before that building was erected. Mr. Perry told me, "I planted them deep, so they would stand up to the wind." In the decades that have ensued, they have done that. I think he would be proud to see that what has become of his saplings; they are now taller than the school itself.

*****

A math teacher went to Father Tribou with an unusual request: He wanted time off during the school year, perhaps six weeks' worth, to take a trip abroad offered him by an organization apparently dedicated to the disruption of a school. Father T, of course, nixed the trip. Apparently the teacher was undeterred. He went. What Father T said to this fellow prior to his departure, I don't know. What I do know is that he took his grades with him. Not only was CHS faced with finding a substitute during the spring of the year, but it had no grades for 150 or more math students for the third quarter. Not even old hands on the faculty accustomed to his creative problem-solving could have guessed Father Tribou's solution.

Father T made an announcement to those students whose grades were missing: "At your lunch period today, before you eat, go to the auditorium.

Mr. James Perry's diligence, dedication, and sunny disposition endeared him to a generation of CHS students.

There you will find Mr. Marczuk and Mr. Moran. Mr. Marczuk will have all report cards of those of you whose last names begin with letters A through L. Mr. Moran will have the cards of the rest of you. Get in the line that corresponds to your name. When you get to either Mr. Marczuk or

Mr. Moran, tell him your name. When he finds your report card, tell him what grade you believe you made for the quarter in your math class. Be honest. Do not lie. That is all."

As I sat in the auditorium waiting for the bell to ring that would bring a flood of students into the room, I had to wonder at the wisdom of this latest brainstorm by our principal. It was true that all report cards were due to be distributed in a couple of days, and it was further true that there was no evidence that we'd ever get the grades from the now-traveling teacher. So, perhaps this solution, if we were to call it that, was as good as any other— probably better than throwing a dart at a board with numbers on it anyway. Then came the bell and the students.

Lew Marczuk and I, doing our best stern-teacher acts, shouted at the sophomores as they entered the auditorium that they should be absolutely silent and should be calculating their grades; the process began. The lines went fast. Students had obviously given it some thought. Remarkably, some were asking for grades like "72" and "74," when they presumably could have asked for better.

I did begin to see the canny hand of George Tribou in the system after a while. Lew and I had taught virtually all the lads when they were freshmen, so it wasn't likely that many poor students were going to try to pass themselves off as A types. And I do want to laud the honesty of the boys that day. For the most part they acquitted themselves admirably. I asked Lew later if he felt that much inflation took place with the boys whose cards he graded. He thought not. I can only remember one exception.

A lad stood before me—call him Bart. I had taught him freshman English.

Bart said, "Ninety-three, Mr. Moran."

I said, "Try again, Bart."

"Really, Mr. Moran, ninety-three!"

"Try again."

"Eighty-five?"

"Again."

"Eighty?"

"Done."

*****

The aforementioned Lew Marczuk was, according to one of his students (who later became the principal of Catholic High, Steve Straessle) "an evil genius." It was a comment meant as sincere praise. Lew was the gigantic stumbling block for most freshmen in terms of making the adjustment from grade-school expectations to those of high school. He taught World History with a passion, and woe to the student who didn't catch at least some of that passion with regard to studying for Mr. Marczuk's class!

Lew was a CHS and Harvard grad who eventually became a lawyer, but while he was at CHS and attending law school at night, he created one of the memorable CHS traditions: the *Time* magazine project. Lew wanted each student to take a different year and to research it as if it were a one-time issue of that famous magazine, covering all the important events of the year. It was THE monumental job for a second-semester freshman, and Lew expected him to devote most of his life to it. No doubt some didn't give it a serious try, but for many the effort they put forth stands out in their minds as the most work they ever expended on any one thing while in high school. With the perspective of adulthood, those who survived and even thrived doing this project are probably grateful for Lew Marczuk's rite of passage.

*****

Brother Richard Sanker has spent a quarter-century ministering to the boys of Catholic High. He has taught French, Spanish, and Religion. He has also excelled as guidance counselor and advisor to boys seeking college entrance. He has been the Rockets' most faithful fan, showing up for virtually every athletic contest in which they have been involved. The only blot on his otherwise stellar record is his penchant for puns. He inflicts these bits of word trickery on both the innocent and the unsuspecting. He expresses no apparent remorse for the pain he causes. One day I hoped to cure him by giving him a powerful dose of his own medicine. Said I, "What description of Gandhi would be apt if you knew that he possessed extremely coarsened hands from manual labor, was very susceptible to injury, and was upset about his bad breath?" I figured if his pun-filled mind could figure out this one, there was no hope for him. But it couldn't. Let the healing begin!

"A super-calloused, fragile mystic, vexed by halitosis," I replied. Though shaken and perhaps even stunned by the atrocity, BRS, as we know him, was not sufficiently realigned by the moment, and he persists to this day with his infamous behavior. It may take an intervention of a stronger sort to convince him to get rid of his bad habit—lame pun intended.

*****

S.H.A.R.C. is an acronym for Sunny Hills Athletic Retirement Club, the brainchild of my Holy Souls and Catholic High classmate and friend Bill Mooney. Before it was shut down after a run of several years, S.H.A.R.C. was to touch the lives of several CHS faculty and alumni.

Former athletes are often reluctant to hang up their…equipment. We were in our mid-thirties when Bill first called me and wondered if we could get together some guys and form a city league basketball team. Not being yet totally undone by the ravages of time, we decided that we could. When we cast our net for players, it was more important that they be congenial teammates than experts in the sport. So Bill and I recruited pals from the class of '61 such as Mike O'Malley, John Matsek, and Joe Smreker. Then I looked to the CHS faculty and found willing participants in Don Lawson, Richard Althoff, Dick Heien, Steve Wells, and Phil Granberry. We also recruited some younger lads from the alumni: Tim Finefield and Dennis Lee among them. What we all had in common was the pleasure of playing the game and the camaraderie, though as all you sports fans know, those characteristics rarely translate into victories.

S.H.A.R.C. became a staple of the lowest level of the city's roundball league, and it's probably true that most other teams smelled a victory when we appeared next on their schedules. We did have some memorable highlights though. Since I was the oldest, I was the team captain by default, and when we played a group of young athletes representing Blue Cross/Blue Shield who were tearing up the league, my teammates looked at me with astonishment when I told them, "We're going to press these guys from the opening tip."

There wasn't any speedy impeachment process available to remove from office a captain who was certifiably demented, so my pessimistic teammates gave it a try. About three minutes into the game we were ahead 8-0, and the Blue Cross guys were calling timeout, screaming at each other that they were losing to a bunch of "old guys." That they eventually drubbed us does not detract from my memory of a moral victory.

Proving that every S.H.A.R.C. has its day is the fact that on one night we memorably (in our minds, at least) upset the number-one team in the league. It was a game in which we played far beyond our individual capacities, leading the usually front-running Coca Cola team from the start. The Coke guys caught us by the end of regulation, however, and any observer familiar with the two teams would have reasonably said that the soda boys would undoubtedly win it in overtime. Such an observation would have been wrong. Chalk up one for the "old guys" from CHS.

*****

In four decades of teaching at Catholic High I can not recall one circumstance of real disagreement that I had with a sister or brother teacher or staff member. When I mention the cordial, supportive, even loving work atmosphere of CHS to others not of the school, they find it hard to believe. Granted, we teachers are not rubbing elbows with our co-workers all day long, but there is more than that to explain the unified environment. I believe that every year that I taught at Catholic High Father Tribou spoke to us about teaching as a vocation, just as his priesthood was. I also think that we who heard him believed him. To influence the world to come through teaching is sometimes more easily imagined than experienced, but if one teaches long enough, he or she is bound to get feedback from adults who were once one's students. The gratitude expressed by them is payment enough for the tests composed and graded, the corrections that had to be made, and the uncertainty that one occasionally has as to the good that one is doing. When a faculty and staff come to sense this appreciation from former students, it galvanizes us to try to continue to do well and harmoniously our work together—and that is what I experienced at Catholic High.

CATHOLIC HIGH GUYS:

Counting the boys I've taught in Religion (thirty minutes each day) and adding them to the fellows I've taught in the 50-minute classes comes to a total of about 175 boys a year. Forty years of teaching therefore amounts to daily, in-class contact with 7000 students, some of whom would be counted twice or more since they were in more than one class with me. Then, too, as the guy in charge of attendance for twelve years, when boys returning to or leaving from school had to give me a note regarding their absence, I encountered many boys whom I never taught. That's a lot of interaction with teenaged males, and I enjoyed it to the last day. As I administered my last semester examination in 2008 and realized that the last few minutes of my career were coming to an end, I marveled at the fact that the boys of 2008 were so similar to the boys of 1968. They were still bearing down, as they first did forty years before, giving that semester test the old high-school try, and they were, as four decades ago, my students of varying talents and inclinations, but still very much Catholic High boys.

I've been fortunate to teach in a school where learning has always been respected by the students. Catholic High School never at any time seemed like anything less than a place devoted to its religious and academic goals. The boys who go there and have gone there have always sensed this. Our Catholic mission, "To teach as Jesus did," has always been honored by faculty and accepted by students. I am very lucky to have been part of this school and to have met so many outstanding boys, who later became outstanding men. The following are some of the things I remember about those boys.

*****

In my first year of teaching, when I had the entire sophomore class all to myself, probably 185 of them, our literature texts were four: one for essays, one for short stories, one for drama, and one for poetry. I taught six classes a day and hoped to find reading selections that would generate positive responses. A dull entry could make for a very long, tooth-pulling kind of day, especially if the volume at hand was poetry.

I assigned my fellows "The Ballad of the Oysterman," a narrative poem by Oliver Wendell Holmes that told about the title character falling in love with a young woman who was separated from him by a river, one that he swam in order to see her. I thought the poem's appeal to the students would be the danger involved (not only the rigorous swim but also that the gal's father didn't like suitors), and the love angle, and the fact that it had a dramatic conclusion—a sure-fire winner.

After I was reasonably certain that everybody understood the poem's details, I decided to ask for a reaction. I chose a lad named Lewin Williams, an outgoing fellow who I was sure wouldn't be shy about expressing his views. He wasn't. He shook his head vigorously from side to side as he spoke negatively about the work. It was a vigorous thumbs-down decision for "Oysterman."

As I sought out Lewin's reasoning, I got one of my first reminders about something that I had probably forgotten in the ten years since I had been a sophomore: Logic isn't always the first line of reasoning for a fifteen-year-old.

"So why didn't you like it?"

"I don't like oysters."

*****

It is to a bee that I owe one of the most heartfelt compliments I ever received from a student. In American Literature class one spring day in 2007, the bee made its way through an open window at the back of my classroom. While its flight was somewhat pokey, its trajectory was straight—at me. As one of the boys was reading a poem aloud, the bee came right down the space between two rows of desks—destination: teacher!

I was not the only one who saw him. Scott Langford, a student in the first desk of the row just in front of my lectern saw it fly by, heading for the human target. I swatted at it with my book, and, amazingly, managed a hit; it fell to the floor at my feet, wriggling—and angry? I stepped forward and crunched him underfoot.

My audience of one looked at the dead bee and then at me. In a tone calculated not to disturb the student who was reading, but with some real admiration, he uttered this one-word encomium: "Dude!"

A couple of days later I told a class of seniors how I managed to evoke "Dude!" from a junior. It was within minutes of this unadulterated bit of self-promotion that another bee, as if on cue, made an entry into the classroom. Instead of heading for me, it aimlessly droned about, a circumstance that inevitably led to a class disruption as otherwise stalwart fellows cowered or semi-seriously attacked. I tried to continue with the class, but I knew until the bee either left the room or was rendered harmless I was waging a futile battle.

Then I saw it headed for me. I paid it little mind at first, perhaps thinking that the odds were against another frontal assault. But advance it did, suddenly landing on top of my lectern and the very book I had used against its cousin. With little forethought and no other weapon available, I pounded it with my palm, and it flipped off the lectern, dead on the floor.

"Dude!" they bellowed.

*****

For me, the following falls under the heading "Questions Too Profound to Answer." A less-than-studious lad happened to catch Sherlock Holmes fever. What inspired his interest in the famous sleuth and the Baskervilles' hound I cannot say, but it was apparent to me from his talk about the book, both in class and out, that he had experienced that "transport" that authors wish they could inflict on every reader. Thus he was prompted to inquire about the protagonist: "Mr. Moran, was there really a Sherlock Holmes?"

"No."

"Why not?"

*****

In my early years at Catholic High I looked forward to the Faculty vs. Varsity basketball game, played after the regular season was completed. As I had been a Rocket myself and was still young enough to play, I expected the game to be fun, especially since it was common for the 800-seat gym to be packed for the occasion.

It was at the spring Faculty-Varsity game of 1969 when a famous fan paid a visit. Muhammad Ali was in attendance for reasons about which I'm still not certain, though perhaps it was to see Herbert Mumford play. Herbert was the Rockets' best player, and he had completed his illustrious career but for this last game. It's possible that Ali, in town for some other reason, heard about our star and came to see him. In any event, word spread quickly that we had a celebrity present, and as we were warming up I saw fans congregating around Ali for autographs. Among that crowd that managed to get the champ's signature was a basketball-crazy youngster by the name of Tim Ezzi, who himself went on to star at CHS, and later he coached our team to many a great win, especially the 2008 state championship victory over Conway—our first in the seventy-eight years of the school's existence. Tim has that autograph to this day, laminated and a bit worn, but a keepsake from that night forty years ago.

As to that night's game, I recall nothing of the outcome (which likely means we teachers lost—as usual), but I do remember being astounded at the ease with which Herbert dominated the play. He seemed effortless as he leaped to sink jump shots and layups or grabbed one rebound after another. Herbert could, as we came to say later, "sky." One play in particular stands out to me. Somehow it happened that I had a breakaway layup. I recall the pleasure of being ahead of the pack as I drove in for the two points. It was at the last second that I realized the ball I had just flipped up in the air to kiss off the backboard for two points had been batted into the stands by the high-jumping, apparently-faster-than-I realized, skillfully-timing-his-leap Mr. Mumford!

To say that the "check" (as we old-timers called it) of my shot into what seemed like another zip code brought delight to the gym packed mainly with students is to say less than the occasion deserved.

*****

The first class I taught, the graduates of 1971, asked me prior to that year's Faculty-Varsity game to help them generate enthusiasm for the contest by making what amounted to an advertisement for it. CHS has long had a closed-circuit TV studio, capable of broadcasting the morning announcements, showing special programs, and filming occasional events such as spelling bees—and ads for the basketball game.

The specific fellows who were putting together the ad had created the name for themselves, the Buffadonx, a crew of about a dozen who were responsible for creating skits for pep rallies and leading cheers at football and basketball games. They asked me to meet them at school a few evenings before the game to tape the ad, which consisted of having a varsity player or two boast about how badly they would pummel the faculty and yours truly to represent the teachers.

The questions they put to me were easy on my ego: "Mr. Moran, what would you say is the strong point, besides you, of the faculty team?" and "You were an excellent point guard for the Rockets, is there anyone of the

Extracurricular activities, such as being on the staff of the '88 *Rocket*, often forged lasting bonds between students.

seniors who can possibly guard you?" I was happy to speak humbly, such insightful inquiries having been raised, and I looked forward to the showing of the ad the next morning.

The following day, I, with my thirty-five homeroom sophomores and the rest of the school, saw the ad as it followed the morning news. The familiarity of the content didn't lessen my attention as the part came for me to be interviewed. "Mr. Moran, what would you say is the strong point, besides you, of the faculty team?"

I was trying to recall my exact words just before they were repeated onscreen, but I was quickly disconcerted to note that though I was answering the question, no words were coming out. I was jawing away, to no effect. It was as if I were pantomiming. What had gone wrong with the sound?

"You were an excellent..." as the sound came up for the next question I realized I had been Buffadonxed. My reply to that question, as well as one or two others, had also been squelched, much to the enjoyment of my homeroom charges, and, no doubt, of the other hundreds throughout the school. I think that now, from a perspective of a few decades, and given the flattering nature of the questions, I can see that when the Buffadonx silenced me and brought a big laugh to their mates and surely stirred up interest in the game, that it was a fair exchange...though at the time I wasn't quite so philosophical.

*****

In some years Father Tribou would put the lowest achieving students in a class together for all their subjects. Whether this had any firm foundation in pedagogy, I don't know, but when he did so, I commonly asked to teach English to that group.

The sophomore bottom twenty-five fell to me one year. One thing that could be said for such grouping: It did away with any posturing. The boys knew what they had in common and didn't try to dress it up. "Dummies" was their most common description of themselves; as I saw it, my job was to get them to abandon that kind of thinking. Their brutal self-appraisal had one benefit that I wouldn't have foreseen prior to teaching them—a brotherhood. Their status, or lack of it, seemed to bring them together— sometimes in ways I couldn't anticipate.

One reason that I asked Father Tribou to assign me to such classes was that I had found out over the years that I always found the boys in them likable. That's not to say that they were always cooperative or even friendly. But they commonly had a kind of forthrightness and lack of pretense that I admired. And they were funny!

Trying to get these lads to write was sometimes a challenge. I had read about an exercise that another teacher recommended for such reluctant scribes. The teacher who invented or had come across it claimed that the writers were enthusiastic, and the results on the readers were positive, so I decided to give it a try. Each student was to get twenty-four sheets of notebook paper, one for each member of the class except himself. He was to write the name of another student at the top of the page. He was then to write something "good" about that student. When he finished, he went to the next sheet of paper and wrote another student's name, then something positive about him, and so on until he had done this for all twenty-four of his classmates.

My students' objections were immediate. "That's too much paper for one assignment!" "How can I write anything 'good' about…?" they joked. I met their protests with this: "Look, you guys, I'm going to give you four points for each page. That means if you do all twenty-four you'll have 96 points. I'll throw in four points for good looks; it's an easy one-hundred percent."

Despite the complaints, the bribe was sufficient. They then wanted to know what I meant by "good." "Anything nice that you can sincerely say," I said. "And it must be in a sentence—at least one." They were mollified somewhat, and I told them they had to sign their names to each sheet, so the guy getting it would know who wrote it. I gave them a few days to put it together. In the meantime I bought twenty-five paper binders for a dime each and with a black felt marker wrote a student's name on each. I hoped the collection of twenty-four pages might seem more important if it was gathered together.

Came the day of delivery, and I recognized that there was some excitement in the air. I held off the distribution until nearly the end of class. Finally, it was time. "Everybody got his twenty-four sheets?" I asked. They were quick to point out a couple of their fellows who were still furiously scribbling, but even they soon raised their heads and looked at me with anticipation and a bit of impatience, as if to say, "Get on with it, Moran."

The distribution of the papers was wild, as I had no organized plan in place. So they were up and out of their seats and hollering out each others' names, and somehow they finally got it done. I passed among them, giving out the paper binders and making sure each boy got his two dozen sheets, as they immediately began to read.

I've never known moments any quieter in a classroom of twenty-five boys than those that followed the distribution chaos. The bell was soon to ring, so I just let them soak up the commentary. When I had walked among them, I tried to see if I could get a glimpse of what was written. I saw only two that I can recall: "Your black Converse high-tops look good" and "Your jokes are sometimes funny." If that was typical, then perhaps the positive effect would be minimal, binders or no binders. The bell rang for lunch, and the boys departed without their usual semi-sprint. One or two joshed each other about what they had written. But it was relatively quiet. I feared an anti-climax. Perhaps the "good" comments hadn't been very spirit-enhancing.

Then I saw that one boy was still in his desk. If any one student in the class was the outsider, he was it. The others, who could be so painfully honest, had more than one unflattering nickname for him (though their use was verboten in the classroom) based on his somewhat odd appearance. His head was down, as if still reading the papers. Then I heard him sob.

I walked to him slowly, fearing the worst. Had the others turned on him, refusing to say something good? Then he raised his head. A smile spread across this face, and he said, "This is the happiest day of my life." It was one of mine, too.

*****

Don Lawson, an excellent teacher of history and my colleague and friend of twenty-five years, is the sort of man who when he tells me that something happened, I know it happened. So, I know this happened. Our main study hall's location has ping-ponged from time to time during my forty years. For a time, the cafeteria did double-duty. In those days we had tables that sat four, as at a restaurant. Keeping order in a study hall when students are sitting alongside and across form one another at close quarters is no mean feat. That was Don's job at third period every day—enforcing Father Tribou's ideal of a proper study hall: perfect silence, no sleeping, and all students actively studying.

The proximity of the students to each other wasn't the only problem. Since the cafeteria is located just off the main lobby, virtually every visitor to the school plus any students passing by were sure to draw the attention of those whose backs were not to the hall, thereby distracting them and subtracting by at least one-third from Father T's study hall ideal. This meant that for Don it was necessary that he patrol the room on foot, perhaps being able to snag a sentence or two at a time from a book in his hand. It boiled down to high-alert guard duty.

One day Don saw a visitor that had escaped the notice of the huddled masses. It was harder to notice than the usual pedestrian wandering by because it was avian: A bird had flown into the study hall. Its altitude was high enough that it drew no notice as it made a circuit, and then a second one about the cafeteria. Don was preparing for the worst: The study hall gang was about to violate two of the three objectives the principal had for the place (though they would be awake!). Chaos was about to ensue. Then, as the bird began its third voyage about the room, and as Don braced himself for the worst, a hand shot up into the air and caught the bird in mid-flight. With no ado, the student looked at Don and then tilted his head in the direction of the lobby and the open front door through which the bird had entered. Don nodded, and the boy rose from his desk, as students commonly did who had been given permission to ask someone a question. So far, no one else seemed to know what had just happened. Holding the bird, which was silent, by his side, the student left the study hall, and, once out the front door, he tossed the intruder heavenward. He then returned to his seat. This feat went unnoticed by all but Don. And you can believe him; it happened.

*****

I had a friend, also a CHS alum, who had moved to Kansas and was teaching high school students there. He called me one night, and while we were talking about teaching he happened to mention that his school, which had about a thousand students (compared to CHS's 700) had six National Merit Finalists. The designation of Finalist is given to students who excelled on the Preliminary Scholastic Aptitude Test when they were juniors. Finalist recognition, if it comes, occurs in the senior year. I've long believed that these finalists are such from the moment that they walk in the door in their freshman year. I don't think high schools "make" finalists. At the best, we encourage and feed their talents, but we're not responsible for them. So my response to his datum was to say that it was nice for the students to be so recognized. At that point he asked, sounding a bit doubtful, if CHS had any finalists. I said we did. How many students attended CHS now, he wondered. I told him seven hundred.

"How many finalists did you have?" he wanted to know.

"Sixteen," I responded. The line went silent for a moment.

How many seniors had we? "One-hundred-sixty."

Again the silence. "Ten percent of the senior class?"

Yes.

And finally, "Wow!"

A lot of bright freshmen walked in our doors one day in August 1983 who eventually became an important part of the class of 1987, of which, I proudly and shamelessly add, my son, John, was valedictorian.

Speaking of John, I figured his life at CHS would be easier the less it was emphasized that we were father and son. I did teach him Latin when he was in the ninth grade and Religion for nine weeks when he was a junior, but we kept a low profile in that area. As a matter of fact, our connection was so subtle that about midway through his senior year one of his classmates asked me, "Are you and John related?"

*****

A famine was sweeping Africa. Oxfam, an emergency supplier, noted for its success at getting food to starving people, was appealing for donations from the United States. I asked Father Tribou if we could have a one-day, school-wide collection to send to the charity. He thought it was a good idea.

"How much do you think we can raise in one day?" he wondered. Where my reply came from, I do not know. "Three thousand dollars," I responded.

He smiled at my bold guess and opined that we might get a third of that. "You'd have to get almost five dollars per boy to get three thousand," he figured.

Assemblies, whether for intramurals, pep rallies, or student elections, have played a key role in creating brotherhood.

He permitted me to announce the collection on TV during homeroom on Wednesday after regular announcements. I decided to give the boys a target at which to shoot. I told them of my $3000 prediction and Father Tribou's doubt. I acknowledged that he had far more experience with these matters than I did. I asked the boys to do what they could.

On Friday, each homeroom representative walked up and down the rows of his homeroom with a sack into which any donations were dropped. Freshmen tend to have little walking-around money, and sophomores aren't much better off. The juniors and seniors bore the brunt of my hopes. Several boys had been assigned to count the collection. Shortly after lunch I heard their report: After a last-minute contribution that was credited to the ROTC department (and which I always believed was a personal gift of Colonel

Jack Hennelley, who ran the ROTC), the total was $3010. I have never been prouder to be associated with the boys of Catholic High School.

*****

One student I taught in two different classes, call him Larry, had more than once expressed to me his admiration for the inventiveness of those who perpetrate scams, or con games. I told him that if he was aspiring to emulate such fellows it was my duty to try to set him right.

"No, no, Mr. Moran, you've got it wrong. I don't want to be one of 'em, I just enjoy hearing how they take advantage of greedy people." I wondered aloud if all victims were greedy. "All the ones I'm talking about are," he countered.

He then told me with some pleasure how a gentleman of his acquaintance had just sold a violin to a wealthy Hot Springs resident for $50,000. Larry claimed that the seller hadn't actually proclaimed the instrument to be a Stradivarius, but that when he had the violin built by an expert forger of old musical instruments, the name Stradivarius had been placed inside. Presumably the buyer had seen it.

"Now, Mr. Moran, you know that a Stradivarius is worth a lot more than $50,000, and the guy who bought it does too. But he thought it was stolen, and so he got it for a lot less than what it should cost. He's a greedy guy, and he deserves everything that happens to him." I don't recall having much of a comeback to Larry's version of rough justice, and I wish I had, because I did have to wonder later if he hadn't taken to heart some of the principles of the con man.

In his senior year, Larry approached me one day after school, with a conspiratorial tone in his voice. "Mr. Moran, you know So-and-so, don't you?" He had named one of his classmates. I told him that I did. "Well, do you know that he's been sick a lot this year?" I told him that though the boy wasn't in one of my classes I had heard of his illness. "Well, Mr. Moran, some of the other guys and I are putting together some money, and I want to know If you want to come in with us." Larry and his pals were, I thought, going to buy their classmate a get-well present.

"Mr. Moran, we're going to take out a life insurance policy on him just in case he dies, with us being the beneficiaries, of course. Want in?"

If I had failed to denounce scammers strongly to Larry before, I tried to make up for it with a wave of condemnation of the entire process, and I called Larry and his cohorts several unflattering names in the process. He wasn't especially offended, it seemed, and simply replied, "OK, I get your point."

I never knew if Larry and the others took out the policy—I don't even know if such was possible, but I am happy to report that So-and-so recovered entirely and has lived a long and fruitful life. Sadly and ironically, the last time I saw Larry he had obviously suffered some serious health setbacks, but at last word he was still with us.

*****

Before the advent of computers at Catholic High, both for classroom and administrative use, our system of assigning boys to class consisted of Father Tribou's summertime sequestering of himself somewhere in the building away from his office (to avoid interruptions) so he could figure the whole thing out. He had long tables with piles of papers distributed on them in a fashion that only he could grasp. One of the results of this "system" was that the boys knew to which classes they had been assigned, but we teachers didn't. So, prior to the first day of school, all a teacher would know was, for instance, that one was teaching a fourth period World History class, but not the names of any of the students in it.

I don't think Father T had a list either. He had simply made up the individual schedule cards for 700 or so students and then trusted them to find their way to the classes to which he had assigned them. That meant that on the first day of school, each teacher had to get the names of the students from the students. What seemed like a logical way to do this, simply passing around a sheet of paper and asking the students to put their names on it, had its shortcomings, especially for new teachers. If a trusting new teacher took that list home with him or her and then proceeded to make a class roll from it, he or she might find it deficient the next day.

When that roll was called the next day, the teacher was almost bound to find thereon names he or she had faithfully copied from the list the night before, such as "Chuck Roast" and "Ben Dover," the very recitation of which would set off gales of laughter in the classroom. Thus it was that veteran teachers counseled rookies to give one small index card to each boy for him to write his name on it.

It doesn't seem to have occurred to many students that this process had a flaw: If a student wished to attend a class other than the one to which he was assigned, all he had to do was to make sure that he went to the other class at the same time period as the one he was dodging, and signed up for that class instead of the one to which he had been appointed. One student certainly figured this out, a fact that was not revealed, however, until the night of his senior banquet, after all his classes had concluded, including the final exams. At the senior banquet, the "I remember when…" part of the program consists of the reading of papers that seniors composed a few days before the end of school, which are usually recollections of humorous events of the previous four years.

It was at that banquet then, that a senior revealed that for both his junior and senior years he had been assigned to one teacher and had instead opted to join the class of another. It was because of this revelation that the following year Father Tribou had all teachers on the first day of school inspect the schedules that he had made out, to make sure that no one had employed the ruse perpetrated by the student the previous two years. As a matter of fact, the change in the system that required checking each schedule evolved into a practice informally known among teachers by the name of the student who brought it about. It was the "Joe Blow Rule." But by choosing to make him anonymous here, however, I'm engaging in some tit-for-tat: His name is once again not being written—this time by a teacher.

*****

Father Tribou once created an English class of seniors who had the lowest averages in the class. He assigned that group to me. I asked him for a good deal of latitude in teaching them, and he obliged. I'm sure my students and I must have done some traditional work with our British Literature book, but what I remember best is the one quarter that I offered to let the boys explore their own interests and to grade themselves.

What I required in both cases was a written explanation, first, of what one proposed to do for nine weeks in the way of exploration, and then, when it came time for assigning one's own grade, I told them that they would have to write me a justification or explanation for the grade. As you might guess, these options, especially the one about giving oneself the grade for the quarter, left a number of my fellows just a bit giddy.

But they soon discovered that planning their own course for nine weeks wasn't as easy as they might have thought at first. My role was to be the interrogator: " What resources are you going to use to find about Babe Ruth? How many books do you plan to read? Are you going to use *The New York Times* microfilm in the library to read about particular games he played?" In other words, I was still a pain but just of a different type—or in a different place.

After some starts and stops, though, everybody seemed to have a course plotted. Some of their projects I can still recall. One boy had a script that his father had written as a young man that he had hoped might become a radio drama, but it never did. The boy enlisted the help of some of his fellows, and they were going to make a recording of the script to give to the boy's surprised father. Another group decided to start a newspaper of its own—none was a staff member of our school paper *The Cicerone*, but they found the idea of their own medium appealing. The name for this counter-publication was a combination of the letters of their names: first, last, middle—who knew?

It turned out to be *JONDALJOK*, if my memory of its spelling and all-caps look is correct. The news guys elected an editor, and he and they discussed stories that they thought *The Cicerone* didn't cover, and then they divvied up the writing and the layout work, and off they went.

A third group project was to make a TV show. I don't think any of the guys had any studio experience as members of Father Frederick's crew, so there was some after-school instruction from Father Fred that had to take place before anything could get televised. One of the boys was apparently an expert at karate, so they decided to showcase his talents on the program.

I don't know if that quarter in "English" class was of much benefit or not, but I do recall some moments of genuine enthusiasm, perhaps a bit more than a Shakespearian sonnet could have generated. The end results were satisfying to me, and, I hope, for the boys. The radio show did get made, as did the board-breaking karate program. *JONDALJOK* appeared in several mimeographed issues that were distributed mostly to other seniors. The paper and all the projects were presented to the class, and they took time to experience and appreciate each other's efforts. Then came the time for grading.

It probably won't surprise you that most of the fellows, in their written explanations to me of why they assigned themselves the grade that they did, tended to do better that quarter than in any other nine weeks the rest of the year. One explanation is still clear in my mind. Perhaps its brevity accounts for it—or its honesty: "I'm giving myself a 93 because I bet my sister five dollars I'd make an A in English this nine weeks."

*****

More than once did Father Hebert organize a school-wide spelling bee that would be conducted on our closed-circuit television network. Each English teacher was to find his or her top two spellers to represent the class. I decided that rather than hold a customary stand-up bee to find my two finalists, I'd save some time by trying something I saw in *Reader's Digest*.

Under the challenging title "So You Think You're a Good Speller?" was a list of twenty words. The article asked the reader to identify those spelled incorrectly and to remedy any mistakes. The answers on the following page actually boiled down to a single answer: All the words were spelled correctly! I thought this would be a good, speedy way to make my selections, so I handed out a list of twenty-five correctly spelled words and gave the same instructions.

When I checked the results, the first one that I found that had no corrections was that of my best student. Well done, grade A student! The second paper that had no corrections, and the only other, was from what might have been my worst student. He had written on the sheet, "Heck, they all look right to me."

And so I had my two contestants. All the top spellers were announced the day before the bee itself was to be held, and more than a few listeners were astonished at my unlikely entry. The fairy-tale end of this episode would disclose that an improbable upset victory by You-Know-Who took place, but, sad to say, it didn't work out that way. As a matter of fact, he didn't show up for the bee at all—said he was "sick." Maybe so.

*****

It was in one of my first years as a teacher that I swore off inflicting corporal punishment on students, a vow I almost kept. The incident that prompted my aversion was not especially physical, but it could have had an ugly ending. As I was doing my peripatetic best to be interesting by making rounds up and down the rows as I taught, I was, of necessity, carrying my heavyweight anthology as I went. As I passed near one fellow, I noted that he had just finished chatting with the lad one row over. Without giving any thought as to all the possible results, I popped him on the top of his head with my textbook. I was surprised by the loudness of the sound as his top and bottom teeth were driven together by the impact. A thought flashed into my mind: "What if his tongue had been in between his teeth? Would I be trying to pick up the perhaps still wiggling tip of it off his desktop or simply be trying to stanch the flow of blood from his mouth?"

That's all it took to turn me into a believer in non-violence as far as treatment of students was concerned. I can recall only one exception to that promise. Some years later, as I was walking down the corridor on the second floor, between classes, with lots of student bodies in motion, I was alerted by a hubbub and an extraordinarily rapid movement of bodies. The opening stage of a fight had commenced. When I arrived, a blow or two had landed and the combatants were still vigorous in the pursuit of their goals. I stepped in between them, presumably thinking that the sight of my august presence would immediately quell the combat. Instead, one of the pugilists, either unaware of my presence or indifferent to it, gave me a solid shot to my right shoulder. That's when I broke my vow—I slapped him, hard, right on the jaw.

The other combatant had previously suspended hostilities when I intervened, and then the fellow whom I smacked said, "Oh, Mr. Moran, I'm sorry!" Perhaps I, too, should have apologized, but I don't remember that I did.

When the class of the two wranglers held its twentieth reunion, I was invited to attend. As I walked up to the location of the reunion, the first alumnus I saw was the fellow whom I had slapped. His first words to me were, "Mr. Moran, do you remember slapping me?" To which I replied, "Yes, do you remember hitting me?" I could tell from his surprised look that he hadn't.

*****

The dramatic and unexpected state basketball championship that the Rockets won in 2008 brought joy to CHS fans. Given the 78-year drought in basketball, the victory was especially invigorating. That victory brings to mind other great achievements by Rocket squads in virtually every sport that the boys in purple and gold have attempted. Our physical fitness teams have won two national championships, and state championships have come in football, soccer, swimming and diving, and golf.

But my sometimes contrarian view of things presents for your consideration another Rocket contest of which we who support the Rockets should be equally proud.

It was an outmanned Rocket football team that took on the Wildcats from the north side of the river not so many years ago, a CHS team that ended up on the losing end of a score that would have taken eleven touchdowns to undo. The defeat was total, crushing—humiliating to some. A week or so after the game a letter about the game appeared in the local paper. The writer mentioned that he had seen the game as a casual observer rather than a partisan. He noted the lopsided score and then ended the letter with nothing but praise for CHS. The team, he said, never quit; nor did the fans. He said that the fourth quarter support for and effort by the team matched that of the first period. I think that game deserves to be remembered for its players and fans who exhibited the never-say-die spirit that one wants to think that our athletic program promotes as an ultimate value. Win or lose…go, Rockets!

*****

One year Father Tribou assigned me to tutor at the last period of the day, which we called Activity Period. One of my tutees (a word used in educationese) was a senior, whose major academic deficiency, I thought, was the result of a lack of confidence. One problem might have been the contrast between him and an older brother who had a sparkling academic career at CHS. The boy's ambitions seemed fuzzy until one day I asked him, "If you could take a trip anywhere in the world, where would you go?" From someone who rarely had much enthusiasm for anything, his immediate reply, full of conviction, startled me: "Australia!"

When I asked him what was so appealing about Australia, the most pertinent thing was that he had an uncle who lived there, and it had always been his dream to go. "After you graduate and save some money, what would prevent you from going to Australia?" I asked. He shrugged his shoulders as if to imply that while he had no answer, the likelihood was nil. It was perhaps two years after his graduation that we crossed paths, and as soon as he saw me his eyes gleamed with a look I hadn't seen before, accompanied by a ready smile, and he proudly proclaimed, "I went to Australia!"

I was astounded. If you had asked me if this lad would have ever ventured to do such a thing, I'd have given huge odds that he would not. As he responded to my request for details, I could see his pride, and well deserved it was, for making the trip. He not only visited Australia, he stayed there for some months at a job working for his uncle. In his manner of the telling was a new sense of self that I hope has not diminished.

I remember many times recommending a book to my students, especially hoping that some underachievers might latch on to it. The book's title *Is There Life After High School?* states the crucial question—and the resounding answer is "Yes!" In the young man I met that day, I saw the effect on a boy who dared to follow a dream—an awesome sight.

✳✳✳✳

Sometimes students get sleepy at school. We all remember that struggle to stay awake. (Well, some may not recall a struggle because they never really put up much of one.) Don Lawson had a study hall to watch at the end of the day. He saw a sleeper and was on his way to bring him back to the land of the awake when Father Tribou, who was passing by and noticed the sleeper, intervened. He signaled Don to hold off.

Father T disappeared for a minute and then returned with an air horn. The lad with his head on the desk was in for a mighty surprise. Delighted students eagerly anticipated the blast of the horn as Father T moved to close proximity. The horn shattered the silence of the study hall, and the lad deep in the land of Nod…barely stirred! He lifted his head slowly, and presumably saw the source of the blast and the priest wielding it; he then proceeded to put his head back down on his desk.

When a high-tech means to solve a problem fails, a method from a simpler time can be re-tried to see if it still works. When last seen on that chilly day in February, Rip Van Student spent the rest of that study hall period standing—outside, at the flagpole, in his shirtsleeves, probably awake.

*****

Given the right circumstances, one can learn a lot in a study hall. I think I learned a good bit in one of mine. My first study hall assignment in 1968 was sixty or so fine young men, mostly seniors. The heat of September was upon us all, and the study hall following lunch was just too much for some. One fellow slept every day. I tried subtle ways to keep him and other the boys awake: walking past and bumping them with a book or giving what I would call a "gentle" tap with my shoe to an exposed ankle. No histrionics. No drama.

But this guy was starting to get on my nerves. I'd wake him, and five minutes later he was gone again. He was a big boy, heavyset, lumbering. My unkind thought about him was "big, fat slob." I never called him that, but it crossed my mind on many occasions. Day after day I'd be at his desk four or five times a period. I really resented his laziness. Then his name came up one day at lunch. Before I had a chance to spout off about his lethargy, Father DeBosier had the floor: "This boy comes from a very poor family. He pays his own tuition. Each day after school he works at an ice house from four to nine, hauling one-hundred-pound blocks of ice. He's a remarkable boy."

Thus did Father DeBosier teach me my first and most memorable lesson about snap judgments about students.

*****

Speaking of that study hall, it provided me with my first occasion to deal with a mutiny. In my rookie year, I had not only never taught a class before, but I certainly never had to ride herd on five or six dozen inmates in study hall who were not inclined to be impressed by a guy in glasses who was the new kid on the faculty block.

Dealing with talking and sleeping students kept me busy during the first few days, but then the weather turned really hot, and the situation deteriorated. The study hall was then located next to the library at the north end of the first floor. When the temperatures soared, Father Tribou had a gigantic floor fan placed in the front of the study hall. The diameter of its blades was over a yard wide, and they stirred up a good bit of air, but the main beneficiaries sat within ten or fifteen feet—and many guys were twice that far away.

It was with the fellows in the back of the room that the trouble started. My "authority" was put to the test one sweltering day when a chant, perhaps unrehearsed, began. "We want the fan! We want the fan!" demanded the denizens at the rear. Their volume increased as they began again. I feared the disruption was about to engulf the school. I had visions of Father Tribou arriving on the scene, silencing the mob with a glare and banishing me to sit in his office. What was I to do?

Suddenly I acted, surely without reflection. I looked into the crowd of chorusing malcontents and picked out one, perhaps the burliest of them all. I grabbed him by the collar and yanked with the full power of my 150-pound (really!) frame and began to "drag" him in the direction of the fan. The surprised bruiser went along for the ride, and as we got to the fan I barked at him. "On your knees!" which he surprisingly obeyed, and the fan, about six inches from him, blew noisily and powerfully in his face, his hair flying in all directions.

Buoyed by my exercise of power, I turned and screamed at the mob, "Now who else wants the fan?" Not wanting to have anything to do with a teacher who was on the verge of a breakdown, the boys quietly returned to their work, and I left the kneeler at his position for the remainder of the period.

This success, if one could call it that, was soon undermined by another intuitive act that had not as fortunate an outcome. In that same study hall was a door that led to a classroom. The priest who occupied that room asked me to watch over his boys one day while he went to the doctor. "I'll just unlock the door," he said, "and you can look in on my boys from time to time." I wasn't sure it would be as easy as he made it sound, but I agreed to help.

I was ping-ponging between my study hall of sixty and his room with its thirty-five students throughout the period. Once when I stepped into his room I heard a radio playing—the sound of which quickly stopped. "Who's got the radio?" I demanded to know. Nobody volunteered. I asked again. No response. "If you don't confess, I'm going to punish everyone," I unwisely declared. Nobody would own up to it. So, good to my ill-advised word, I made a blanket writing assignment that I announced was due the next day— and that there would be dire consequences if the work wasn't done.

Generations of Catholic High seniors recall the Ring Mass as the event that bound them to each other and to Catholic High.

After school, driving home, I was troubled by the encounter and my decision but determined to see it through. I stopped at a grocery store and saw that Ken Lipsmeyer, one of the boys who had been in the room that I had disciplined, was sacking groceries. He was probably the only boy in the class whom I knew, as his sister Norma had been a classmate of mine at Holy Souls. Here was somebody who would tell me the truth since we were outside the realm where the schoolboy code of never ratting on a fellow student held strong.

"Who had the radio?" I asked, as he helped me tote my groceries to my car.

"Mr. Moran, there was no radio," Ken assured me.

"I heard it clearly," I countered.

"I'm pretty sure you heard the radio of a car that passed by on Lee Street," he explained.

"Are you sure?" I wondered.

"Yes, sir."

"I feel awful. I gave everybody all that punishment work," I lamented.

And in a sentence that at one and the same time made me feel much better and much worse, Ken said, "Oh, don't worry about that work, Mr. Moran. Nobody is going to do it anyway."

*****

CHS has had exchange students at least since 1960, when our class welcomed Gerd-Theo Umberg who was from Neuss, Germany. Gerd's English was first-rate, and remains so, as I have conversed with him by e-mail. One of our recent exchange lads was not as fluent as Gerd and frequently got assistance from his classmates. This boy decided to join the football team, and one of our coaches invariably greeted him with "What's up?" His sole response was "Not much" until a teammate decided to provide him with an additional reply. As the "instructor" looked on with great anticipation, the next encounter between exchange student and coach went like this:

"What's up?"

"My wiener, Coach."

That unexpected reply provoked an immediate, angry response: "Who told you to say that?"

Our guest turned to his language advisor and said, "Him—the fat one, Coach."

The follow-up fate of "the fat one" can be readily imagined.

*****

Some students' words, both written and spoken, will probably stay in my mind for a long time. They are as varied as the fish of the sea. I fondly recall some here:

"Mr. Moran, did you ever give a student a 100% on an essay?"

"Yes."

"Did it hurt?"

*****

When I made it clear to my students that I didn't carry a cell phone, one was prompted to ask, "Do you have electricity?"

*****

When I asked Alec Baldwin (the student, not the actor) if he could provide an example of "a non-contradictable statement," a phrase we had just read in our text, he responded, "Mr. Moran is a genius." "Good answer!" said I.

*****

A student whose voice was as unwavering and flat as any I ever heard asked about a word we had just read, "What does *monotone* mean?"

*****

A junior was confused by Scott Fitzgerald's choice of an abstruse word: "What's the definition of laundry?"

*****

One of my writers was describing what sounded to me like a daunting job in a Mexican restaurant: "After the diners are gone, I pick up their bowels from the table."

*****

Another writer was identifying one of the salient characteristics of his much loved Jeep: "It has an 800-pound wench on the front bumper." Unable to resist, I red-inked in the margin, "No room for her in the Jeep?"

*****

The computer has certainly made writing much easier. It has also created problems that the old-fashioned way didn't entail. One of my lads was describing what I'm sure was intended to be a "glistening" lake. But when he applied his spell-checking tool to the essay, it obviously didn't recognize his spelling and offered an alternative—which he took. This is my explanation for how a senior came to write the sentence, "The lake was glycerin."

*****

One of my students asked me to proof-read his college essay, the only assistance that I offered on such efforts. I refused to suggest idea to improve the essays, thinking that the work should be the student's own. The question that he was to address in his essay was essentially "Why do you want to go to this college?" Though the college was in Boston, this Little Rock lad was keen to attend, and his essay indicated that he was well informed about the school and truly desired to join the student body. It was written with passion and commitment. Clearly he had worked hard to answer the question and wrote his response carefully. When I handed it back, he was startled. "Wow, Mr. Moran, you haven't marked a single mistake on the whole essay!"

"It was excellently written, but there *is* a mistake: I think you'll stand a better chance of being admitted it you don't spell *Brandeis* wrong every time you write it."

He made the corrections and is today an alumnus of Brandeis.

*****

The longest essay I can recall a student writing was Tim Bordsen's thirteen-page, encyclopedic discussion of why rabbits make the best pets. Tim was obviously an animal fancier, and he loved the works of James Herriot, the British veterinarian who wrote such books as *All Creatures Great and Small*. After graduating from CHS, Tim took a trip to England, where he went to the village where the author (whose pen name was James Herriot) lived, called him, and was invited to come visit. When Tim later told me of the encounter with the famous man, I couldn't help remembering that magnum opus about rabbits.

*****

I can't count how many times I took up notebooks over a forty-year career. Yet one instance of doing it sticks with me. It was an English class of sophomores who handed over their work. I graded it, and on the day I returned it I got a bit dramatic. I was most unhappy with the overall effort and didn't hold back from saying so. At one point I grabbed a notebook and said, "This is what many of these notebooks deserve!" At that point I hurled it disgustedly into the wastebasket. Point made, sophomores? I figured so. At that juncture I gave back all the notes with a last admonition to all the wise fools that despite the poor quality of the notes, they would be needed to study for future exams so they should be saved.

The following day a lad in that class approached me with a small, rectangular blue piece of paper in his hand, the CHS absentee slip. Obviously he had missed the previous day. He inquired, "Do you have my notebook? I understand you gave them out yesterday." I was stumped, for just a moment, as to where it was. When I realized its last location, I said, "I'll have to give it to you tomorrow."

That afternoon, having waited perhaps thirty minutes after the last bell, thereby hoping to cut down on the number of student sightings of my humiliation, I made my way to the back of the school and prepared for my first episode (and, to date, last) of dumpster-diving. I can't remember how I got into the gigantic garbage can, but I can recall that as soon as I got there I wanted to get out, ASAP. The odor of the container was assaulting my nostrils, and my hope to find the missing notebook faded as soon as I assessed the mountain of trash. But the gods who watch over thoughtless teachers were with me, as I quickly managed to find the notebook no more than a foot deep into the pile. When I returned the notebook the next day, I hoped that it didn't have the olfactory essence of its overnight repository still attached. Note to self: be less demonstrative.

*****

For some boys, getting through Catholic High School or any other for that matter is a struggle. When I announced my resignation at the graduation of 2008, I thanked, among others, the students present and past who had inspired me by their willingness to put up that struggle. I have known too many such boys to cite them all, and I don't want to single out any by name, though some may be obvious from the details I present in this appreciation.

We have had boys in wheelchairs who needed assistance to go to the bathroom. I praise not only them for their persistence in the face of a challenge but also their faithful friends who assisted them. I honor the boy who, from a local testing center, finally got a diagnosis for his learning problem; he happily, even proudly, told me he had a reading problem known as dyslexia, which was a great relief from what he had believed until that day. His third grade teacher had told him: "You have a black spot on your brain." *Dyslexia* sounded a whole lot better to him than that, and today he is an alumnus.

Another boy was hit by a brain fever that threatened his life; yet just a little over a year later he proudly attended graduation exercises to get his CHS diploma. I was also inspired by the blind student who learned how to get anywhere he needed at CHS, as well as the deaf lad who sat in the front row doing his best to read the lips of his teachers. I also recall the challenge faced by those who stuttered and who spoke up nonetheless. Young people bravely bearing burdens provide an uplifting example.

Overcoming physical obstacles was paralleled in the lives of boys whose struggle was against something unseen: family or personal problems that somehow were put aside long enough to get through that period known as "high school." I salute all who held to the course despite the winds of adversity. They are prominent among the Catholic High boys whom I am proud to have known.

*****

Robert Anderson of the class of '80 told me that he and several of his CHS classmates meet for lunch from time to time. Tales from their high school days invariably come up, and one was recently recounted involving two classmates, call them Mark and Steve.

The duo was heading home—late, or very early, depending on how you judge 3:00 a.m. They were attempting to reduce the time getting home by propelling their car at a speed higher than was optimal for safety. Then they hit a parked car.

It was, as noted, three o'clock. The street was deserted—no witness in sight. "What shall we do?" one asked the other.

Even at seventeen, there is no doubt that each could easily list most, if not all, the consequences of owning up to the deed. If they just put their car in motion and continued home, a tale could be concocted on the way to account for their own dented vehicle (somebody hit the car in a parking lot and then drove off—yeah, that's what happened!). And that would eliminate all the repercussions: an upset owner of the other car, raised insurance rates, perhaps a ticket for unsafe driving, disappointed (or worse) parents.

"You know what we should do," was the reply.

They exited the car and walked to the house in front of which the damaged car was parked to knock on the door.

Robert Anderson said that on hearing the re-telling of this story, one of his classmates said, to the agreement of all present, "That's what Catholic High was all about."

FATHER GEORGE TRIBOU:

Father George Tribou was Catholic High's mainstay for five decades. Emerson said that an institution is often best understood as the "lengthened shadow of one man," and that seems an apt way to sum up Father Tribou's influence on CHS. My memories of him are from my youth and various stages of my adulthood. His presence is still powerful in the lives of many of us who learned much from him in boyhood—and beyond.

*****

After basketball practice one afternoon in December of 1960, having left the gym, I went into the school to get books from my locker. There in the hallway Father Tribou stood, as if waiting for me.

"Mike, I need some help. Will you call your parents and ask them if I can drive you home after you've assisted me? Tell them I'll see that you get supper." Would I help my senior English teacher and the vice-principal? You bet! To get me to a phone, he led me to his living quarters, a room off the first floor of the building at 25th and State. As I entered his room, one I'd seen only once or twice from the corridor, with a desk by the door and lots of books on the wall opposite, I saw sitting in a chair a bedraggled kid—maybe fifteen years old. I nodded to him as I dialed the phone Father T had handed me. My mother sounded as surprised as I was to hear of the request, but she quickly agreed to it.

Then Father Tribou introduced me to the boy, whose name I don't recall. But I do remember Father T saying, "Mike, take this boy to the barber shop. It will be open until six, and the barber is expecting you two." The shop was a couple blocks from school, though it wasn't one I'd ever used. The comment caused me to look closer at the fellow. His hair was shaggy, especially by the popular flattop and burr haircut standards of the early sixties. He didn't look too pleased about the marching orders but made no protest. Before he and I took off, Father T took me into the hall and closed the door, the boy still in his room.

"He has run away from home in Pennsylvania. The juvenile authorities here picked him up and called me after he told them he is Catholic. I'm going to send him home tonight. Tell the barber to give him a haircut like yours." Mine was pretty much a burr but for a bit of fluff at the front. I guessed that my partner might not be too happy about the style.

I never saw a grimmer face on a person getting a haircut than that boy's. I'm sure the only reason he didn't run away again on our way to the barber shop was Father T's promise of a "delicious" meal after we got back—he looked like he could use some food. And delicious it was; one of Lido's finest. Lido was just a few blocks from CHS at the foot of Main Street, and it had a reputation for fine food. The lad looked even more out of place than I did, as his grungy blue jeans and flannel shirt were not the style of most diners at

Father Tribou and Father Frederick established a priestly presence that positively influenced thousands of boys.

Lido. After the supper was over, we piled in Father T's car, and he headed for what turned out to be the Greyhound Bus terminal.

Father Tribou bought him a ticket home, somewhere in Pennsylvania, and handed him a five-dollar bill just as he was about to board the bus. Throughout all, the haircut, the dinner, and the trip to the bus station, the boy had given semi-surly, monosyllabic replies to just about every question put to him. I had decided early, on the way to the barber shop, not to waste any effort trying to get him to talk. He wasn't having any of it.

But when he got the money from Father Tribou, he broke a bit, smiled, and thanked him more heartily than I would have imagined possible until it happened. He got on the bus and rode away. Father Tribou took me home.

It might have been thirty years later that I thought to mention the night to Father Tribou. It was still vivid in my mind. "Remember that kid from Pennsylvania that you put on the bus?" He looked puzzled. I reminded him of more details. Still nothing. "You took us to Lido!" I asserted. No bells. It's fair to say that Father T wasn't good at names, but he could usually remember very specific details of dealing with boys. Nothing I could tell him ever brought the situation to mind. He had completely forgotten it.

When I taught "Tintern Abbey" by Wordsworth in the years after Father Tribou's death, the story about the runaway boy and what Father Tribou did for him came to me as the best example I knew that matched Wordsworth's description of "those little, nameless, unremembered acts of kindness and of love" that he was using to describe "that best portion of a good man's life." And that fits to a T the "best portion" of Father T's life as well.

*****

One important thing I learned in forty years of teaching is the sometimes-not-appreciated fact that there are different kinds of flatulence. The "Oh, excuse me!" type is completely forgivable. The "Hey, how about this!" genre is altogether different. To master the classroom, a teacher has to develop judgment regarding the two, for to ignore the wrong one is to invite chaos, while commenting on the other needlessly embarrasses an innocent party.

A priest at the old school was presiding over a study hall when type-two made itself present. I once read that such "crepitation," as Father Tribou (having found a relatively elegant synonym) was accustomed to call it, is most enjoyed by children and prisoners of war. I know of no proof of that assertion, but it's somewhat persuasive to me since various CHS denizens seem to possess some of the characteristics of both groups, thus suggesting they would be especially appreciative of the phenomenon. The priest who had been subjected to the sub-sonic boom was sure that he knew who the perpetrator was (often the body language of those in his area will give him away). Apparently the priest didn't want to discipline the lad on the spot—perhaps coping with the ongoing hilarity of the others was his major objective. So he sent the boy to see Father Tribou, who handled most discipline matters with which others didn't want to deal. The priest's parting words were, "Be sure to tell him what you did!"

As he slowly made his way to Father Tribou's classroom, the boy decided that he couldn't bring himself to use any of the slang terms for the act—it was just too embarrassing. How was he to explain himself? Just before he faced the stern taskmaster, the golden words came to him. He wasn't literally facing Father T, for the priest was alone in the room at his desk and grading papers, giving the boy at his side only a small percent of his attention.

"Why are you here?"

"Father So-and-so sent me."

"What did you do?" said the half-attentive priest.

And the just-remembered description flowed, so much more acceptable a way to identify the deed: "I broke wind."

As a result of not listening closely, Father Tribou's reply must have left the lad in a world of wonderment: "Well, go get a broom and sweep it up. Then bring a dollar on Monday to pay for a new one."

*****

As principal, it fell to Father Tribou to make a lot of announcements on the intercom. Surely the more announcements one makes the more likely becomes the possibility of saying something unintended.

We have a CHS tradition that goes back at least as far as my time, and it has been variously known as the Outside Reading Selection and, more recently, the Book of the Month. These works are both fiction and non-fiction; they are additional required reading for all students, and for many years students bought them in the office each month from the secretary.

One month the freshman and sophomore selection was Walter Lord's non-fiction account of the sinking of the Titanic. Father T went to the office microphone and made this announcement: "It's time for the Outside Reading Selection. Ninth and tenth graders are to come to the office and see Mrs. So-and-so for *A Night to Remember*. Don't forget to bring your three dollars to pay her for it."

*****

Another announcement that he made more than once had to do with one of our foreign-exchange students. This lad from Eastern Europe had one of those last names that you'd think a man like Father Tribou, accustomed to the likes of Zakrzewski and Chwalinski, would not find hard to pronounce. But the fact is the boy's name eluded him. So when Father T called him on the intercom, it was always this way: "See me in my office, Martin from Poland." Among the students the name, as you might imagine, stuck.

*****

One of Father Tribou's traits, that of being candidly direct, won him a lot of appreciation in the community, where more diplomatic men of the cloth were the rule and not-so-novel. He was prized as one who would give memorable invocations at banquets, so unpredictable was his choice of words and ideas. He would say startling things about the person being honored or the crowd present, such as asking God to withhold his righteous hand from smiting an individual or group so sinful. Many listeners liked the unexpected from Father Tribou.

Father T told a story once of confronting one of Little Rock's wealthiest men with such candor. Witt Stephens, a highly successful businessman, was known to gather interesting and diverse groups to lunch with him. Father T was a guest from time to time, and it was at one of these get-togethers that he asked Mr. Stephens if he was familiar with Jesus' mention of the "camel" and the "eye of the needle." Mr. Stephens averred that he was. Father T wanted to make sure.

"You know, Witt, that passage says that it will be easier for a camel to pass through the eye of the needle than for a rich man to enter the kingdom of heaven."

"Yes, Father, I know the story."

"Does the story worry you?" said the famously frank priest.

"It does, Father. I'm afraid that Sam Walton won't get into heaven."

Few of us ever got in the last word with Father Tribou as cleverly as that.

*****

Just before school began each year Father Tribou called a faculty meeting. One subject for discussion each year was the issue of students with special circumstances. These could range from family problems to a boy's being subject to health issues. One year Father Tribou said that he wanted to tell us about a boy with a very serious personal problem and mentioned what it was. Father T then listed the teachers who had the boy for class the coming year and asked them to be aware of the boy's situation. He was about to identify the boy when Father Rossi, who was to be one of the teachers mentioned, spoke up right away.

"Father Tribou, I don't want to know the boy's name. I'm afraid it will negatively influence my treatment of him."

Father Tribou said he understood and asked if any other teachers felt the same. As none did, Father T excused Father Rossi from the meeting so that he could mention the boy's name to the others.

As Father Rossi's Latin class was of two years' duration, the boy was in his class for 360 days. From time to time Father Tribou would kid Father Rossi that he was going to tell him the name of the boy. Father Rossi always vigorously insisted he didn't want to know. On the last day that the boy would spend in class with Father Rossi, the lad in question brought Father Rossi a note from Father Tribou that had been folded and stapled. As the boy went to his desk, Father Rossi pulled the staple, unfolded the note and read, "Ray, he's the one! George."

*****

Father Tribou's name was frequently mispronounced. If one listened carefully to the man pronounce it himself, it was clear that "tribe-you" with the accent on the first syllable was his preferred form. He told us when we were his students that his paternal grandfather sold something from a wagon—perhaps juice—and that he had, as his business calling card, this sign painted on the wagon: "After you've tried all others, Tribou."

*****

In my days as a student at the old CHS we used to joke about the "swimming pool" located there. We could see plainly that no such place existed. The school's gym, however, was real, and it was located on the second floor of a building whose bottom floor consisted of dressing rooms, showers, and toilets. Even though the gym was tiny (and it was much too small for any actual games to be played there, since there was no room for spectators), occasionally it was used for something other than basketball practice.

One such event was a dance during my senior year. It was an informal affair in a less-than-elegant environment, but we lived in an era when dancing was king—anywhere, anyplace, if dancing was offered, we'd show up. So that night, the gym was pretty well jammed with boys from CHS and girls from St. Mary's. Father T, as was his custom, was chaperoning. He used to claim that he was assured of speedy entry into Heaven without visiting Purgatory just because he had listened to so much bad music and seen so many ugly dance styles come and go in fifty years of monitoring dances. Standing on the sidelines grimly observing the proceedings, cigar in hand, he called me over to him. He handed me a key with these instructions: "Go see if the poles are still standing." I had no idea what he was talking about.

"What poles?" I inquired.

"In the room right below this one," he replied. At that point he walked out onto the dance floor to separate a pair of dancers who had apparently crossed the Tribou Line of Demarcation as to close dancing. Left standing

A sight familiar to boys from 1950 to 2001: Father Tribou taking charge of a situation.

there, I contemplated what room was "right below." Surely it was one or the other of the two dressing rooms. There were no poles in either. But he was the boss, and so I dutifully went downstairs, wondering exactly what constituted that room.

As I got to the bottom floor, my estimate of a room just below the gym floor brought me to a door between the dressing rooms that I had passed a thousand times without ever having given the slightest thought as to what lay behind it. I inserted the key; it turned easily. The room was dark, and I fished for a light switch just the right of the door. It was there. I flicked it. The lights flashed brilliantly on the swimming pool! What we all thought was just a figment of many imaginations, a pool that had lain unseen in this place every day of my high school career, was a reality. Next I saw that in the pool, stretching from its bottom to the ceiling above were four telephone-pole-sized columns that were obviously holding up the floor for all the dancers above. (The pool, I later learned, had so many irreparable leaks that it had been shut down many years before.) As my eye went to the ceiling, I thought I could see it vibrate, but I didn't care to spend much time contemplating the implications of the movement. So shocked was I to discover not only the pool's existence, but the props for the gym above, a gym in which I had spent hundreds of hours practicing basketball, I was unnerved. Stunned, I turned off the light and headed back upstairs to make my report.

"The poles are still standing," I solemnly told the cigar-smoker, returning his key. He just nodded matter-of-factly, apparently satisfied that no cave-in disaster would occur on his watch, and he turned his scrutinizing gaze back on the dancers.

*****

For many years I lobbied Father Tribou to include in our Book-of-the Month list J.D. Salinger's *The Catcher in the Rye*. Though it is widely considered a classic and a rite-of-passage text, he and I both knew full well that the language of the protagonist, Holden Caulfield, was anything but uplifting. We also knew that some parents might object to the book on those grounds, though I think it easy to convince a thoughtful, concerned parent that Holden's stereotypical foul language is the least important thing about him. Holden's great heart, his desire to exist in a world of goodness, and his obsession with anything that is "phony" are his signal, worthy characteristics.

For some reason, after many years of saying "no" to my request, Father T agreed that it could be our outside reading selection for juniors and seniors. I'm patting Salinger on the back, not me, when I say the book has been a big hit. Not every lad, however, is taken with Holden. I've heard some interesting feedback about his deficiencies in class discussions, but the praise for the book far outweighed the negative comments.

A year or so after Father Tribou died, *Catcher* was handed out in class as the next month's book. One boy, on taking it home, must have mentioned it to a parent who was quick to call an English teacher to object. This, approximately, was their conversation:

Parent: "Why is Catholic High promoting such a filthy book?"

Steve Wells: "It was the last book that Father Tribou added to the reading list."

Parent: "Oh, all right then."

*****

Father Tribou told a story about when he was a young priest and received an emergency call from one of his students who lived near the old school, asking him to come to the boy's home. A terrible family fight had broken out, and the boy's first impulse was to call Father Tribou. Apparently both of the boy's parents had been drinking, and Father T arrived when the hostilities were still ongoing. The boy let him in, and Father T could hear from a room in the back of the house the sound of cursing, and of things being broken, and punches being landed. When he got to the room where the fracas was taking place, his presence did not immediately calm the two bloody and disheveled combatants, who continued to hurl family possessions and insults at each other.

The young priest, on the first such call of his ministry, eventually began to have a calming effect on the quarreling parents, however, and they ceased open hostilities. After a time, and some counseling being given, and some promises having been made, Father T thought it safe to leave the boy and the battlers alone. As he made his way through the house back to the front door, he noticed for the first time that at the entrance and exit to every room was a small holy water font, a miniaturized version of those at the door of Catholic churches, and commonly associated with the homes of the most pious of Catholics, who blessed themselves with the water whenever entering or leaving a room. He said that he hated to think how bad things might have been in that house without the beneficial effects of holy water.

*****

A boy from the class of '85, call him Alan, would probably acknowledge that we on the faculty gave him our full attention; he was that kind of young fellow—lots of energy, some of which needed, in our opinion, re-directing. I imagine sometimes Alan must have felt as if he was getting more "attention" than he thought he deserved. Sometimes it must have felt as if we on the faculty were watching his every move.

Alan was in New York City, according to the story I heard, during a time when school was out: at Thanksgiving. Alan had actually left school a day before the Thanksgiving break, ostensibly to attend a church function. Somehow he ended up in New York! As he stood on a corner in Manhattan, he felt a tug at his arm.

As he looked in the direction of the tug, he saw Father Tribou, who said only, "Alan, you'd better behave yourself while you're here. I'm keeping an eye on you." And then, as suddenly as he appeared, Father Tribou disappeared into the crowd. Of course, Alan was surprised—if not astounded.

Back in Little Rock and at Catholic High the following Monday, when Alan first laid eyes on Father Tribou he said, "Boy, Father, I was sure surprised to see you in New York."

"When did I see you in New York, Alan?"

"Last Saturday, on Fifth Avenue."

Father Tribou looked at him quizzically. "I've been in Little Rock since school let out, Alan. You must have seen someone else."

Now Alan knew a thing or two about putting another person on, so he decided to check on Father Tribou's whereabouts with two reliable sources, those bastions of truth and champions of honesty: Father Frederick and Brother Richard.

"No, Alan, Father Tribou did not leave Little Rock over the vacation. He was here the whole time," was essentially what he heard from each. What Alan made of this triple denial isn't known, but one can speculate that he might well have entertained the notion that his eyes and ears had played tricks on him. What else could he assume, given the testimony of the Triumvirate of Truth?

Students are adept at putting things over on their teachers; some, like Alan, raised the practice to a high art. But when a trio such as the aforementioned decides to collude and conspire against a single student, that boy, even if his name is Alan Crook, doesn't stand a chance.

*****

The Rocket football team had an away game at Cabot. It was the custom of the host school to send complementary tickets to the visitors, and CHS had gotten an allotment of about thirty. Father Tribou put a notice on our faculty bulletin board that teachers could request a ticket. I had no intention of going, but a colleague, knowing that, asked me if I'd get a ticket so he could pass one on to a friend. I agreed, and Friday morning I went to Father Tribou's office before school. My feeble rationalization for the undeserved ticket was that I wasn't actually going to claim I was going to the game, though the request was certainly an implication that I was.

"May I have a ticket to the game?"

"Of course. Say, since you're going, would you be willing to give me a ride?"

What could I say? He then invited me to have supper with him before we left. I agreed to that as well. Five-thirty—sharp!

I returned to the faculty lounge, ticket in hand, and sought out my expectant fellow teacher.

"I'll see you at the game!" I barked.

"What?"

I explained. He couldn't restrain a laugh; I must have looked pretty pitiful.

Whatever plans I had for that night had obviously gone down the drain.

I arrived for supper just at the appointed time. I'd never before eaten with Father Tribou at CHS. Also in attendance were the other two residents at the school: Father Frederick and Brother Richard. The dining room was just a few feet down the hall from where all three lived on the second floor. The cook was Mrs. Flossie Johnson, who also did laundry for the trio as well as some light housekeeping of their rooms.

Father T sat at the head of the table. Across from him on a table beyond the dinner table's end was a television set. Father Frederick and Brother Richard sat along the sides of the table, and I joined one of them there. Father Tribou said grace, and Mrs. Johnson began to serve the meal.

It was a Friday, of course, the night for high school football, and though the prohibition against eating meat on Fridays had long since ended, fish was the entrée at CHS that night—a fried patty of some sort, not one of my favorites. We also had French fries and dinner rolls. No one besides me seemed to notice or care that we were eating an all-brown meal. Not bad in itself, but it seemed odd to me.

After grace had been said and the food placed before us, Father Tribou gave a nod, and one of the black-clad fellows got up, went to the TV, and turned it on. The four of us did not speak. Tom Brokaw of NBC News did all the talking. The meal passed in silence on our part, perhaps a throwback to seminaries, where often mealtimes were characterized by silence on the part of the eaters and spiritual reading was offered for collateral consumption. I asked my two fellow teachers at a later time if that dominance by the

On CHS's 60th anniversary in 1990, the principal and his seniors went to the 25th and State school site for a commemorative photo. (file photo from *Arkansas Democrat-Gazette* by Jeff Bowen)

anchorman was typical. It was, they reported, an unvarying ritual—a thing at which priests excel. Our homogenously hued meal was over before the news ended, and Father Tribou and I lit out for the territory of Cabot.

When we got to the game, we went to the side of the stadium for the Rocket fans, and Father Tribou and I got a seat in the second row, meaning that nearly every person who passed was likely to see him. And many passed. And few failed to notice him.

As I noted before, despite his many intellectual strengths, Father Tribou's weak spot was names. It wasn't as if all names escaped him, but having taught so many for so long, it was understandable that some eluded him. So as we sat, prominently, we would note the coming of a face that lighted up as it recognized the high-profile boss.

"Who's that?" Father T would mutter to me.

"That's Jones, "I'd say.

"Hello, Father Tribou!"

"Hello, Mr. Jones," he'd reply, without the slightest touch of embarrassment that without me at his side he'd have had no clue. Jones, or whoever it was Father T had saluted by the name provided, would respond with a smile at the mention of his name, not knowing that it was yours truly who was responsible for the detail. And me? Did Jones see me, his teacher of English for his junior and senior years ten years before? No! I had become Ralph Ellison's protagonist: *The Invisible Man*. I was Eliot's Prufrock, the "attendant" who was "glad to be of use." I guess I was glad.

Though Jones's name had escaped Fr. T, his memory for other details about Jones hadn't. "Jones's mother had a small restaurant on Main Street many years ago," he told me. "Her husband left her, and she was the sole support of the family. They've had a hard time making it. Jones had a job after school to pay his tuition." That was the kind of memory Father T had—one that grasped the essence of the life of the boy who had been under his care.

So after the filing in for the game and the halftime parade to and from the concession stand were completed, my identification duty was pretty much over. We watched the game and cheered on the Rockets. The ride back to LR was not likely punctuated with post-game analysis. Anyone who knew Fr T would never consider him a sports fan. But we had a trip's worth of things to say to each other; what we talked about specifically, I can't recall, though it was probably about detention hall or a student's problems, or student essays. Father Tribou's thoughts and conversations seldom strayed from school—it was his life.

So at this late date I'm admitting that I was part of a scheme to acquire a free ticket, but if I hadn't, I'd have missed out on a memorable evening, including that monochromatic supper.

*****

Father Tribou had every right to expect those of us who were his teachers to make it to school despite adversity, given the fact that he held himself to that standard, and then some. (Though it's fair to say that he lived closer to his work than did most of us.) As he aged and as health problems beset him, he was dogged in his determination to show up every day both to teach and to run the school. After having been hospitalized for one surgery, he returned to school in mid-morning and was sorting the mail, as was his wont, by noontime; he was in the classroom the following day. He was a very tough guy!

I worked in the attendance office for twelve years, and that meant that

I took calls in the morning from parents reporting their sons' absences. Teachers who were forced to miss school soon learned that I was at the phone by 7:30, and it was then that most called to report if they were unable to come. Their desire wasn't so much to talk to me as to avoid talking to Father Tribou, whose tone of voice on hearing such news was usually unhappy. So when a teacher did call me and report his or her absence, I was forced into what was one of my most unpleasant jobs: telling Father T that someone was missing for the day. He invariably was agitated, and on more than one occasion I reminded him not to kill the messenger.

He was an equal-opportunity responder, however, when it came to a teacher staying home with sick children. When I would tell him a man was absent for that reason he would ask, "Why can't his wife stay home with the child?" When a woman teacher called in for the same circumstance he'd say, "Can't her husband stay home?"

Teachers were so aware of Father's impatience with absences that they took pains to avoid it. Our present principal, Steve Straessle, came in to teach for the afternoon after one of his children had been born in the morning. Others brought their sick children with them to school rather than miss teaching.

Perhaps the most extreme case I can recall of Father Tribou's attempt to inculcate in his faculty his devotion to CHS above all else was his question to a faculty member who had just informed him that he would be missing school to attend the funeral of his grandfather: "Were you *close* to your grandfather?"

*****

MICHAEL J. MORAN   139

The last words I can remember Father Tribou saying to me were actually the first words he said when I knocked on his hospital door. Unknown to me then was the fact that all my other visits to his hospital bed would occur after he slipped into a coma. But when I did hear him speak, Father T thought I was a hospital employee come to put him through a procedure he was obviously dreading, for he said when I was still outside the door, "Are you the devil?" When I entered, I assured him I was not, but I can testify that his wicked humor was intact to the very last.

As Father Tribou approached death, some of us who visited him thought that he was still aware of the outside world even though he didn't speak. Steve Wells was at his side holding his hand while speaking about Martin Luther King Day. Father Tribou had been adamant that giving school children the day off to celebrate Dr. King's life was sending the wrong message about the man. He told us that he read of a birthday celebration for Dr. King by some of his associates that occurred during the work day, and that after the songs were sung and the cake cut and eaten, Dr. King told everybody to get back to work. So during his time as principal, Father T would have a speaker come to CHS on Martin Luther King Day and tell the students of Dr. King's significance in American history—but there was no day off at CHS.

Accordingly, Steve was telling Father that it was MLK Day and that CHS was still in session—despite what all the other schools were doing. Steve said at that point that Father Tribou's grip tightened, as if to acknowledge the news.

I had a similar experience when I took a copy of John Knowles' *A Separate Peace* to read to him. Father T loved the book, and he and I sparred about it for years, as I thought it was badly written. "Moran, that just shows how bad your taste in literature is," I recall him saying to me after I had criticized the book. He once copied for me an article that Knowles had written about the book and all the money that he had made from it over the years. Father T enjoyed rubbing it in that my opinion was in the distinct minority.

So I thought that if he could hear anything, that he'd want to hear from Knowles rather than me. I told him I was reading it under protest and then read a few pages. He showed no response until I said, "Well, I guess you've heard enough for one day." At that point he squeezed my hand. I didn't know exactly what the grab meant, but I thought I did, so I read him a few pages more.

When Father Tribou died, his funeral was held in the CHS gym, of course; actually he had two funerals, one for students and their parents and the other for the general public. My most vivid memory of the day is that for his final resting place at Calvary Cemetery Father Tribou chose to reside for all eternity next to one of his teachers: Richard Althoff. It seems fitting that these two men, from different generations, who both spent their adult lives devoted to the boys of Catholic High School, should rest together in peace, their jobs superbly done.

Asked once about whether he ever got lonely in his life as a priest, Father George Tribou's response summed up his commitment to his beloved Catholic High boys: "The only time I'm lonely is the day after graduation."

GRADUATION–2008:
(This is an after-the-fact recollection of my retirement announcement
on May 23 in the Catholic High School gymnasium.)

In January of 1961 Catholic High School moved from its State street
location to this campus on what was then called Lee Avenue. My classmates
and I were seniors that year. Practically everything we did for the remainder
of the year was a "first" of some kind or another. I'd like to mention three of
them, all of which took place in this gymnasium.

On Saturday, February 4 the Rockets inaugurated this gym against the
North Little Rock Wildcats. I'm proud to say I was part of the Rocket team
that night. The final score was Wildcats 33, Rockets 34.

On Saturday, April 15 the first prom that was held in this room was a big deal for
me—I had a date! Even better than that, she was beautiful, and she was the homecoming queen. Best of all is the fact that I'm married to that queen, Cathy Wortsmith.

Finally, on Wednesday, May 31 the first graduation from this school took
place. I was one of the speakers that night—my first instance of speaking in
public. Father Tribou said he had a hint for those of us who might be worried
about getting butterflies. I thought I knew what he would say: imagine that the
audience is naked. He didn't say that. He suggested that each speaker should
wear an athletic supporter to calm his nerves. I never asked any of the other

students who spoke if they followed Father Tribou's advice, but I followed it, and it worked like a charm. I was so excruciatingly uncomfortable that hot and humid night that I never gave a thought to my nerves.

Since this gym was the occasion of my first public speaking, it seems the right place for my last occasion to speak publicly. I am resigning from my position at Catholic High tonight. But before I go I want to say something to three groups.

First, to the staff and faculty of Catholic High, past and present, I want to say thank you for your good example—your devotion to the boys and hard work have always inspired me. I also want to thank you for your camaraderie and friendship.

To the parents, both here tonight and to all parents whose sons I have taught, I want to offer my thanks for your support and encouragement. As well I thank you for the time you've given to this school in so many volunteer activities, like the Booster Club, the Auction, and the Junktique Sale. And I thank you for entrusting to me and the other teachers your most precious sons.

Finally to the seniors, tonight's and those from every graduation I've attended here, I thank you for your enthusiasm and energy. They have, in turn, energized me. Thanks also for your effort, your striving to do well. The stage manager of *Our Town* says that it is that "straining away" to make something of ourselves that is our outstanding human characteristic. If you do that your entire lives you will have done well.

So, this is not goodbye, this is *auf Wiedersehen*—until we meet again. Goodnight, Catholic High. Proudly I speak your name.

POSTSCRIPT:

When I retired in May of 2008, the number of faculty members who were CHS alumni dropped from thirteen to twelve. That some of CHS's finest teachers, past and present, have come from outside the ranks of CHS grads doesn't need mentioning. An institution that doesn't benefit from outside influence eventually suffocates under its provincialism. With that being said, I also tout the value of a significant alumni presence on the faculty. Graduates who have taken things they cherish from CHS and then want to return as teachers have much to offer for having absorbed the values of the school.

Not being afflicted with triskaidekaphobia, I think thirteen is a lucky number for CHS in terms of alumni teachers, and I'm hoping that soon one of you boys who went here will replace me to get CHS back to that number. What I can offer you by way of incentive to do this job isn't an enormous amount of financial remuneration (though it is plenty, given a broad view of all the people who work throughout the world). But the intangibles of the job are so potent in their payoff, that once you experience them you will find them so sweet that they are almost unbearable.

These pluses are found in the faces of boys who didn't understand, but now do, because you taught them. They come from the sincere appreciation from parents who believe that you have helped their beloved sons. They are in the words of graduates who generously express thanks for what you did for them. These are benefits that you will enjoy as long as you live.

One of you reading this should listen: Your Alma Mater is calling. Come back and give to other generations of Catholic High boys what you have received—by doing so you can touch the future.

CPSIA information can be obtained
at www.ICGtesting.com
Printed in the USA
FSHW021849140220
67020FS

9 781945 624049